SOMEONE'S WATCHING YOU!

SOMEONE'S WATCHING YOU!

50 STEPS TO PROTECT YOUR PRIVACY

From **MICROCHIPS**
IN YOUR UNDERWEAR to SATELLITES
MONITORING YOUR EVERY MOVE,
Find Out Who's Tracking You
and What You Can Do about It

FOREST LEE

Aadamsmedia
AVON, MASSACHUSETTS

Copyright © 2011 by F+W Media, Inc.
All rights reserved.
This book, or parts thereof, may not be reproduced in any
form without permission from the publisher; exceptions are
made for brief excerpts used in published reviews.

Published by
Adams Media, a division of F+W Media, Inc.
57 Littlefield Street, Avon, MA 02322. U.S.A.
www.adamsmedia.com

ISBN 10: 1-4405-1273-6
ISBN 13: 978-1-4405-1273-5
eISBN 10: 1-4405-2664-8
eISBN 13: 978-1-4405-2664-0

Printed in the United States of America.

10   9   8   7   6   5   4   3   2   1

Library of Congress Cataloging-in-Publication Data
Lee, Forest.
Someone's watching you! / Forest Lee.
p. cm.
ISBN-13: 978-1-4405-1273-5
ISBN-10: 1-4405-1273-6
ISBN-13: 978-1-4405-2664-0 (ebk.)
ISBN-10: 1-4405-2664-8 (ebk.)
1. Personal information management. 2. Electronic surveillance. 3. Privacy. I. Title.
HD30.2.L437 2011
323.44'8—dc22
2011008808

This book is available at quantity discounts for bulk purchases.
For information, please call 1-800-289-0963.

ACKNOWLEDGMENTS

Indispensable to the process of crafting this book were my readers: I'd like to thank Vanessa Lord for her intelligence and editorial wizardry; Bruce Hallberg for his honesty and insight into the world of business and the pharmaceutical industry; and Stacy Kissel for her scientific kung fu. Jess, Amy, and the rest of the staff of Miracle of Science provided a home away from home for this book and its writer; without their omelets, IPA, and free Wi-Fi, this would have been an insurmountable task. If you're ever in Cambridge near MIT, go there. The stools are uncomfortable, but the food is perfect and the beer comes quickly. I owe Cris Concepcion, Christian "Norwegian Love Machine" Baekkelund (also often available in Cambridge near MIT), and Aaron Grossman for the onslaught of e-mails about the various uses of aluminum foil, terrifying household robots, and all the ways in which the Internet is trying to kill me. The Wolfpack has been invaluable for their support and general wolfpackery. Finally, I would like to offer my thanks to my editor Peter Archer for having the idea for this book in the first place, and faith enough in my abilities to let me write it.

"I always feel like somebody's watching me."
—Rockwell

"Gentlemen do not read each others' mail."
—Henry L. Stimson, U.S. Secretary of State

CONTENTS

PART III: SPIES, CRIMINALS, AND CREEPS ARE WATCHING YOU

INTRODUCTION

Can you feel it? That tingling in your spine; the crawling sensation in your skin that means someone's eyes are on you? Everywhere you go, it happens. Strangers on the train stare at you—are they following you? People lurk in alleyways, watching as you walk by—are they sizing you up as a victim? Corporations analyze every purchase you make, tracking your age, gender, spending habits, and even your medical history. Governments peer through your windows, read your e-mail, and listen in on your phone conversations. No one is anonymous, no one is ever alone, and there is no such thing as a secret. Most of what you do is recorded, collated, and filed. You are under surveillance.

We live in a world where privacy has been traded for great deals on today's special; where individuals have sacrificed their freedom for the sake of what feels like safety. Your friends willingly volunteer information about themselves—and about you—for the sake of scoring points in a game or saving a few bucks on their next cup of coffee. The trappings of daily life disguise a host of tracking devices operated by people dedicated to serving your needs—or exploiting your weaknesses.

The currency of the day is information. Nations and economies are founded on it; corporations thrive on it; spies and stalkers will torture, maim, and kill for it. What you consider a single useless fact—your driver's license number, the name of your elementary school—is a bit of data worth hundreds or thousands of dollars. Treasure so valuable kings once rode to war for it sits lightly in your hip pocket.

Information is power. People with power want more of it, and people without power seek to gain it. Whether that means spending vast amounts of time and money collecting and collating thousands of terabytes of data on the movements and behavior of an entire population or lurking in the shadows to learn the secrets of a single individual, people have cultivated the habit of watching one another for centuries.

These days, everyone in the world leaves a trail of information in his wake. Like a buck moving through the woods, your spoor is invisible to the untrained eye, but to a person who knows what he's looking for, it's plain as day. Your trail makes you vulnerable to hunters. It tells them where you've been, hints at where you're going, and tells anyone who looks everything they could ever want to know about you.

Hunters come in all forms. Market research firms sift through mountains of personal information looking for patterns that can serve as leverage to open new markets. Governments scan the crowds for information on dangerous terrorists and dirt on political opponents. Spies pry fragments of intelligence from the smoking ruins of an enemy's computer—or the stiffening grip of his dead hand. Criminals watch and wait, looking for marks foolish enough to display a moment of weakness. Everything of value is eventually found out by someone, and every piece of information in the world has value.

Billions of dollars are spent collecting and analyzing this information. The economy of the developed world is based on this data and develops based on the abilities of governments and corporations to use it to manipulate your behavior. Billions more flow through the black market, tied to your credit card numbers, your mother's maiden name, your passport photo, and your social security number—all lifted without your knowledge by a vast and shadowy network of government officials, corporate shills, and international criminal cartels.

If you're not a commodity, you are a target. Someone, somewhere, is ready to pay for your precious personal data. No matter where you are, someone is watching you.

PART I

CORPORATIONS AND TECHNOLOGY ARE WATCHING YOU

Right now, someone you've never met is thinking about you. There are vast dossiers on you—thousands of pages filled with analysis of your behavior, your likes and dislikes, your mood swings, and drinking habits. A good market research firm knows more about your habits than you know yourself.

This is big business. Every one of us is a mobile wallet stuffed with money that every corporation in the world is competing to empty. Billions of dollars and thousands of hours are spent tuning every product to tempt those dollars away from you.

For the convenience of these corporations, most people willingly convert themselves into a string of numbers. Every magnetic strip in your wallet includes a host of information linked to a vast store of data about you. This information is shared with analysts who use it to predict your behavior. Did you buy a Slim Jim at 2:30 A.M. on a Tuesday? Statistics show an 85 percent probability that your next purchase will be a Mountain Dew. Bought both? In that case, you're probably having fun at home with *World of Warcraft.* Try the new expansion, coming soon!

Your path through the new economy leaves a glittering trail of bits that marketing departments from New York to Cupertino greedily slurp up and process into actionable information. We're a world of consumers. The only things we produce are echoes of ourselves; those echoes are traded like cattle in an electronic black market of psychographic research and targeted ads.

Here's the shocking thing: Most of this information is *willingly* volunteered. You don't *need* a credit card. No one forces you to fill out all those online forms. If someone asks you whether you like an ad or not, there's no reason you need to answer.

But rest assured—even you anarchists out there fit into a demographic bracket. Someone, somewhere, is analyzing your behavior, crunching the numbers, and creating a campaign to sell black clothing and red bandanas to you.

GOOGLE'S PLOT TO CONQUER THE WORLD

Google's unoffical corporate motto is "Don't be evil." And it's a good thing they're not evil, because they know everything about you.

THREAT LEVEL

WHAT IS IT?

Seriously? What is *Google*? Where have you been the past twelve years? Google is everything. It's a noun, it's a verb, I'm sure it's been used as an adjective, and it's probably going to be an adverb (Googly) pretty soon.

Google was founded in Menlo Park in 1998. The company's primary business on the date of its founding was Internet search—a fiercely competitive market. The industry battlefield is strewn with the bodies of high-tech luminaries and mysterious strangers—Lycos, AltaVista, WebCrawler, Ask Jeeves, Yahoo, and Microsoft. Finding stuff on the Internet is big business, and Google is at the top.

Imagine the Internet as a vast junkyard filled with pornography and poorly written editorials in which people call each other Nazis. Buried in that junkyard is a lot of very valuable stuff, but you have to dig to find it. To dig, you need a bulldozer, but you're not allowed to drive the bulldozer. Instead, you have to scream to the driver of the bulldozer what you're searching for and hope he understands what you said over the sound of his engine. What makes it worse is that 10 million other people are also screaming requests at him. More often than not, you're going to end up with a confusing pile of nonsense. That's what search engines were like before Google.

The trick to building a better search engine is to ensure that the software that drives it can understand and interpret a request, even when it is poorly phrased or badly spelled. It's not easy. If you've ever worked retail, you know that most people don't know what they're really looking for. Try mediating that interaction through dumb software and you can see why the people who develop search engine software are hyperfocused, anal-retentive weirdos with a high degree of psychic potential.

Delivering useful information is an extremely valuable service, but making money off it is difficult. Google figured out, like everyone else, that the money's in advertising. Google's innovation was to target ads based on your search terms. Searching for a way to hang yourself? Google has a brand of rope they'd like to recommend. In short order, Google went from being a search engine to being an ad-placement agency. They pay close attention to every term dropped into their search engine.

Google isn't in the business of selling you anything, they're in the business of selling you to their advertisers. The more you use their search engine, the more they know about you, and the more niches into which they can shoehorn ads. They will stop at nothing to make every piece of information in the world searchable. More importantly, those bits of data will be tied to targeted ads.

HOW DOES IT WORK?

Search is based on keywords. The engine adds complexity by also looking at correlations between multiple keywords in order to target results more specifically. If you type *burns* into the search field, you'll get very different results than if you type, *It burns when I pee.*

The engine ranks the results using a piece of software called PageRank. Google won't tell anyone exactly how PageRank works, but the simple version is that it ranks a site or individual page based on how many other pages link to it. Each incoming link is considered a vote for a page. Some "votes" count more than others—if the *New York Times* links to your homepage, that counts more than the link your aunt put on her cat's blog.

The ads on Google's search results page are served by a program called DoubleClick. DoubleClick thinks about your keywords in a different way than the search engine. When an advertiser signs up with Google, he selects keywords and concepts with which he would like to be associated. DoubleClick looks for those keywords in search queries and serves ads based on that. Pretty simple, and not at all scary, right?

Right. Except Google is in the business of improving the targeting of their search results and the relevance of their ads. The best way to do that is to pay very careful attention to who is doing what with their services. Whenever you perform a search through Google's engine, they track your search terms, your IP address (which includes geographic information, just like your postal address does), what web browser you're using, and the date and time. If you click on a link, that information is saved. If you're signed into a Google account at the time of your search, even more information is captured and saved.

The ads served up by DoubleClick drop cookies on your machine that track much of the same data. DoubleClick keeps a log of any ads you click on and remembers you so that similar ads can be targeted at you in the future. This is all done without your explicit permission.

To become one of the nearly 200 million folks with a Gmail account, Google requires a name and birth date, and offers you the option to use something called Web History. Web History, if you opt in, can track every web page you visit and store a detailed history on the Google servers. This data is used to target search results and ads to your apparent preferences.

DoubleClick scans e-mails the same way it does search terms—every e-mail that moves through the Gmail servers gets scanned for keywords. Ads are served based on those keywords to anyone using Gmail. DoubleClick remembers those keywords, establishes trends, and targets ads to individual users based on what they have a tendency to write about.

Taken in pieces, none of this seems terribly sinister. Google's entire corporate persona is based on the ideas that:

- You can make money without doing evil
- You can generate billions by decreasing the sum total of ignorance in the world
- The power conferred by knowledge should be shared with everyone
- Business does not require exploitation or violence

These are revolutionary ideas, and because of them we respond to Google with affection.

But the fact remains: Google wants to know everything about you. They have the capability to build a detailed dossier on every single person who uses their services, a dossier that could do far more damage to many individuals than a single embarrassing e-mail or misplaced instant message. Google is a vast, vertically integrated corporate behemoth—the biggest Internet company in the world. It is a giant that sees everything and never, ever forgets.

WHO INVENTED IT AND WHY?

The primary players in the creation of Google are a pair of geniuses named Larry Page (the "Page" in PageRank) and Sergey Brin (whose name will never be used as part of a product name because no one is totally sure how to pronounce it). They created PageRank and incorporated Google while they were PhD candidates at Stanford.

When they met, both men needed a dissertation topic. To math and computer science geniuses, figuring out a good way to effectively index and search a few trillion unique documents sounds like fun, and so PageRank was born. Page and Brin are idealists who believe that Google's primary mission is to organize every piece of information in the world and make it easily accessible and useful to everyone.

They're good guys who just happen to have invented the most useful thing in a stalker's toolkit since the telephoto lens and chloroform.

WHO'S USING IT TO WATCH YOU?

Pretty much everyone

Google watches you. DoubleClick reads your e-mail. And with your name and one or two other pieces of information, almost anyone can find your address, the names of your relatives, your phone number, your workplace, your vacation photos, and everything else you've ever done or said online.

The Internet never forgets. Usenet—the text-only precursor to the World Wide Web—was created in 1980, and for almost twenty years served as the premier forum for nerds and basement dwellers to insult one another semianonymously. It established the tradition of poor behavior, bad writing, and sophomoric humor that serves as the backbone of Internet culture. Google owns an archive of almost the entire history of Usenet. It is not entirely outside the realm of possibility that your mom met your dad on alt.swingers in 1983, and that Google has a detailed archive of the beginning of the romance between them and their six closest Internet friends.

Former classmates, ex-lovers, kids you made fun of in high school—all of these people have access to Google, and through it, to you. Your friends and your enemies can find you, your boss can track down the pictures from that tequila-and-blow hazed weekend in Mexico, and potential employers can find evidence of your poor sportsmanship on Xbox Live. Thanks to the Internet, you're a public person, and thanks to Google, your skeletons are laid out in alphabetical order for all to see.

WHY IS IT WATCHING YOU?

Google and DoubleClick watch you to learn how to target ads more effectively. The more narrowly targeted an ad is, the more valuable it is, and the more Google can charge if you click on it. Idealist philosophy aside, Google's true business is the same as any other company—they are in it to make money.

The information they collect is also used to improve their search service. If Google knows how you behave online, it can build a deeper understanding of what you mean when you enter certain search terms. Using your IP address, Google knows where you are and can therefore return search results for massage parlors in your neighborhood, rather than just telling you where the most popular massage parlor in the world is.

As for the traces you leave behind on the Internet that Google then picks up and indexes for all to see . . . well, that's information, and all information has value. Someone might someday want to know more about you. Google's purpose is to make sure that person is satisfied.

WHY SHOULD YOU BE WORRIED ABOUT IT?

Google tracks your location and behavior in great depth. Using that information, they could build a detailed dossier. They may not have your actual name, but using the data they do have, an interested third party could easily figure out who you are.

The definition of *evil* in "Don't be evil" is pretty subjective, but we can probably all agree that actually building blackmail dossiers on hundreds of millions of users is at least a little evil. Google doesn't look like they're going to snap and start slaughtering kittens anytime soon, but . . . .

Google is a publicly traded, multibillion-dollar company. If Google were a country, it would be one of the 100 wealthiest nations in the world, playing in the same economic field as Jordan and Costa Rica. Twenty-four billion dollars isn't money. It's a gravitational field, an irresistible force that attracts ever more wealth. A publicly traded company of this size either continues to increase shareholder value or withers and dies. And shareholder value isn't increased by being good. In fact, evil is a proven money-maker.

Many oil companies and cigarette manufacturers didn't start out evil, either. Most of the people who run them now aren't evil. Evil is a pretty rare quality in individuals; it's an emergent property of large organizations motivated by profit. Billions of dollars can serve as an extremely effective blinder to the common good. To avoid doing evil, a corporation must tread very carefully.

The China syndrome

A few years ago, Google launched its search service in mainland China. China has more than a billion citizens, a rapidly growing middle class, and one of the fastest Internet adoption rates in the world. By 2025, China will be the world's largest economy. For a global Internet services company like Google to ignore these facts is suicide.

For four years, Google allowed its search results to be censored by the Chinese government, a government with a long record of human-rights abuses. Google grumbled about the censorship, but they put up with it until they were hacked by someone in China in early 2010. The level of sophistication behind the attack was unheard of in the corporate sphere; the hackers used tactics and tech typically only employed by government or military organizations. They were looking for search engine source code and access to the e-mail accounts of human rights activists.

Google left mainland China shortly thereafter, but it wasn't an aversion to evil that led them to drop China—it was a threat to their bottom line. In this case, the best interests of the Chinese people happen to align with Google's profitability. The question here is, can Google maintain and correlate its profit with the good of the people forever?

WHAT CAN YOU DO ABOUT IT?

Stay off their lawn

Google relies on its users to volunteer most of the information it collects. By visiting the Google website, you sacrifice a certain amount of privacy, in the same way that you do when you enter property belonging to someone else. What you do on my property is, to a certain extent, my business.

The easiest way to prevent Google from collecting information is to simply not go there. Don't get a Gmail account, don't sign on to YouTube, don't install a Google toolbar on your machine. If you must use a search engine, do so from a computer that is not your own and is not operating on your home network or at your workplace.

Every website you use at least captures your IP address. Many more collect other data, through cookies, login information, or by tracking what you click on. The only sure-fire way to avoid this is to leave the Internet and never return. However, this strategy is only reasonable if you live in a cave or in the woods, and are content to avoid all human contact forever. Luckily, there are other steps you can take.

Bad browser! No cookie!

The first and easiest way to foil Google is to set your web browser not to accept cookies. *Cookie* is a delicious name for little pieces of data that many websites leave on your hard drive. The cookie helps the website remember you later. Refusing cookies will hobble some functions on some sites, but it's a small price to pay for increased privacy. You can find your browser's cookie settings in the Privacy or Security tabs of the Options or Preferences menu.

Opt out

Google has been kind enough to develop a plug-in for most popular browsers that opts you out of most of their data collection. It is called, predictably enough, the Google Analytics Opt-out Browser Add-on. Download and install it, and Google will forget you exist.

Disguise your IP address

There are powerful online tools you can use to surf the web anonymously. Services like anonymouse.org and software like Tor are the online equivalent of pulling a bootleg turn in the middle of a tunnel to throw off pursuers. They cast a smokescreen over your activities, stripping the headers from your data packets and bouncing your requests through a series of computers that forget you the second they pass along your click.

Lie

Once you post something anywhere on the Internet, there's a very real chance it will stay there forever. A determined Google search will eventually turn it up. That isn't Google's fault. If you'd been thinking clearly, you never would have allowed your friend to post that picture of you motorboating an underage stripper in Tijuana. But now it's there, and it's not going away.

If you must misbehave online, do so under an alias, using an anonymizing technology. Never post your picture online, and don't associate with your real-life friends. Never volunteer information, and if you have to, lie. Perform searches on variations of your name every few months, looking for evidence that your jerky online personality has been associated with the real you.

When you find something incriminating online, e-mail the administrator of the site hosting the evidence, and ask him or her to take it down. If you can get it taken down quickly enough, it might not be copied or archived anywhere. If the owner of a site refuses to remove pictures or other personal information about you, you may have to complain to his or her hosting service or Internet Service Provider, or even consider legal action.

CHAPTER 2

TRYING TO STAY HIDDEN? TOO BAD. FACEBOOK WILL FIND YOU

What does Facebook do with all of the information they collect on you, and why do they want to set you up with an over-thirty single so badly? Keep a pair of dry undies handy, and read on.

THREAT LEVEL

WHAT IS IT?

Facebook is the current king of all social networks. Five hundred million people worldwide have Facebook accounts. One in three people in the United States is on Facebook. The next most popular social networking website is a Chinese site called Qzone, with 200 million users. Way over in the shallow end of the pool is Myspace, with 130 million tweens and crappy emo bands clogging their pages. Twitter boasts a paltry 75 million users, and every one of them is the most boring human being you've ever encountered in your life. The cool kids are all on Facebook.

You're on Facebook whether you mean to be or not. Even if you don't have an account, several of your friends do. If you've had your picture taken alongside any of them, it's probably online, with your name and face tagged and visible to anyone with access to your friend's photos.

Facebook relies on the tendency of people to brag about the most mundane aspects of their lives. It appeals to our desire for celebrity. A Facebook page is a self-published tabloid, detailing everything about you for all the world to see. It strips away the anonymity of the Internet without relieving you of the courage anonymity brings.

There was a time when people were extremely hesitant to give out personal information online. When creating an online persona, they relied on no one recognizing them. Back then, only your close friends could know for sure who you really were. But Facebook doesn't work unless we're honest. There's no point to Facebook unless people admit who they are. It asks us probing questions, and expects honesty. We give it our name, our birthday, a list of our likes and dislikes, and we share with it our opinions about everything from politics to food. We tell it where we went to school, where we've worked, and what we like to do for fun. We give it our sexual preference and ask it for help finding a date. We show it pictures of ourselves at our best and our worst. Facebook is a total stranger that knows everything about us.

The friends who never leave

Facebook isn't the only stranger learning all about you. People are increasingly mobile; they go to college thousands of miles away from home, take jobs in other states, and occasionally go live the life of an expatriate in some romantic foreign destination. Such a change used to mean losing contact with all but those friends willing to engage in an extended correspondence, even though the chances of seeing you alive again were remote. Moving to another city was like being eaten by bears—your friends would miss you for a short time, but most of them would quickly forget you except as an interesting anecdote.

Now, you can easily reconnect with people you haven't seen in twenty years. Your Facebook friends list is potentially hundreds of people, most of whom you barely know at all (and some of whom you might actively dislike), but they all have access to your most intimate details.

Facebook has a goal above and beyond allowing you to reconnect with all the people you secretly hated in high school. Facebook knows you—sometimes better than you know yourself—and it's determined to keep learning more about you.

HOW DOES IT WORK?

Facebook is far less complicated than Google. Ad service and recommendations made by Facebook are done using simple keyword analysis and a record of your IP address. When you sign up, Facebook gives you a series of boxes to fill in, each of which is simply a collection of keywords. What television shows do you like? What are your favorite books? Are you single? Married? Do you have pets? How old are you?

All of this information is volunteered willingly by members. Your friends have already supplied their e-mail addresses (and access to their e-mail address books), the names of their high schools and colleges and workplaces. Using just your IP address, your e-mail address, and your name, it can instantly offer a pretty solid guess about who your friends might be. Provide it with more information, and Facebook can offer you hundreds of people you probably already know.

As Facebook learns more about you, it will continue to recommend folks who might be (or might once have been) your friends. Through the ever-growing complexity of this network, the site learns more and more about you. Who do you invite to your events? Who do you exchange pokes and messages with? Who do you date?

Since advertising was first invented, marketing professionals have been trying to find ways to weasel this level of detailed personal information out of people. Until Facebook, it never occurred to anyone to simply give everyone in the world a form to fill out—a form that could freely be cross-referenced with their peer group. Facebook represents the most valuable repository of psychographic, demographic, and behavioral data on the planet.

You're not the only person who provides Facebook with information about you. Facebook's advertising partners provide conversion information—if you click on an ad and navigate the advertiser's site for a while, that company could be giving Facebook detailed information about your activities on its site. According to their privacy policy, Facebook keeps that information for up to six months.

Remember how Farmville and Mafia Wars took over your newsfeed before you figured out you could block the application from showing up and annoying you? Remember how you seriously thought about deleting your Facebook page because those games were either more annoying than a fart in an elevator (if you didn't play them) or so addictive that college began to seem like an unnecessary distraction (if you did)? Those games aren't owned or run by Facebook, but they can see your profile just like your friends can, and they propagate like a pyramid scheme. You get those invites to help your friend find a pot of gold or whack some generic videogame Italian because your friend gets points for recruiting you.

Connect the dots

It's not just applications inside of Facebook that pass information about you. Through a program called Connect, applications outside of Facebook exchange information with the social network. Hundreds of websites and mobile applications connect you to Facebook and share your activities with your friends—and with advertisers.

Everything you do on or through Facebook is another piece of information companies use to profile you. Every piece of information you give them is one more thing they use to target ads. Facebook works because we tell it everything there is to know about us.

WHO INVENTED IT AND WHY?

The primary mover behind Facebook is a deeply ambitious young man named Mark Zuckerberg. He wrote the first version of the software that would become Facebook while he was a sophomore at Harvard. It was originally intended as a visual directory for the students of the university, but quickly grew beyond that. Within a year, several other colleges were added to the site's client population. The following year—2005—saw the site expanded to any college or high school student. In 2006, Facebook opened itself up to the population at large.

It is Zuckerberg's vision that guides Facebook's explosive growth, and its hunger for your information. He doesn't view Myspace, Twitter, or the world-famous Qzone as his competition. His sights are set firmly on Google.

If Google's attitude towards information is socialist (free and easily accessible to everyone), Zuckerberg's is anarchist. In interviews, he targets Google's model for information flow as too restrictive. Google may be an excellent research tool, he argues, but the information that truly matters to people is transmitted through traditional social networks—family, friends, coworkers. When was the last time you found a good restaurant through Google? More likely, you got a recommendation from a friend and then used Google to find the address. To Zuckerberg, the recommendation is the high-value piece of information, not the address.

The flow of information through offline social networks—also known as small talk—is what holds communities of people together. You may only have a small number of people with whom you can talk about anything, but the closeness of that group is maintained by consistent communication of less important data: things like movie reviews, book recommendations, and shared recipes.

Zuckerberg believes that the open flow of information between people on Facebook not only creates genuine closeness but that it also creates a self-organizing database of information relevant to his users. His ultimate goal is an environment of free-flowing information that allows people to find what they're looking for before they even start looking. The perfect friends list will ensure that people know instantly where they're going to eat on Friday night, what movie they want to see, and what bar to go to afterward.

WHO'S USING IT TO WATCH YOU?

Your friends

And by "your friends," I mean everyone you've ever known, associated with, or passed on the street. Your mom is on Facebook. Possibly your grandparents as well. Your teachers are on Facebook. Your boss and all of your coworkers are on. The bartender from Saturday night is on Facebook, and so is that cute guy you were too much of a coward to talk to. Your favorite television shows and authors and bands are there. Toys and quirky packaged foods and clothing stores all have Facebook pages. All of them have access to your profile.

Depending on your privacy settings, certain information (at a minimum, your name and profile picture) is visible to any random stranger. By default, much of your profile information is at least visible to friends of your friends. And, of course, whenever Facebook thinks someone might know you, they suggest your name and picture to him or her.

Facebook, obviously

They keep track of what you're doing. Using keywords on your profile, your lists of interests, and the things you've "liked," they target ads at you. You are their most valuable asset, and the better they know you, the more valuable you become.

Also, Facebook's friends

Facebook's advertising partners are keeping track of what you click and when. It's illegal for Facebook to share "personally identifying information" with its advertisers, but it's also tricky to define "personally identifying information." Advertisers receive unspecified user data from Facebook that could include almost any level of detail. Also, all those games you play and all the websites that allow you to share hilarious pictures and videos of cats being just adorable? Those websites can and do track you by name and IP address. While you share LOLcats with your friends, Facebook's affiliates and partners share your information with their friends.

The "Man"

The government just loves Facebook. Criminals tend not to be very bright people, and it turns out some of them love to brag about their crimes. You or I, having just robbed a bank or killed a guy, would be smart enough to keep it to ourselves. That's why you and I have jobs that don't involve ski masks and gunplay. (Unless you're a professional biathlete, in which case, good for you.)

The FBI, Homeland Security, and the INS have created false profiles and friended their suspects. Are you sure that's your grandma who just friended you? If you work on Wall Street, it might actually be the Secret Service, checking to see if you're posting any "special" accounting tips or vacation photos from the Cayman Islands.

Bullies, burglars, and bad guys

Facebook is a potential treasure trove to the criminals and con men that lurk everywhere on the Internet. Every piece of personal information you post online is another building block to your identity. Your name and birth date are passable forms of identification, and the name or location of your elementary school might be the security question you picked when you registered for online banking. Your friends are eager to hear about your vacation, and you're eager to tell them, but posting the details of when you'll be out of the house is an invitation to have your windows broken and all your stuff redistributed through the secondary market.

Why is it watching you?

Facebook pays close attention to your behavior in order to zero in on your personality and serve you ever more highly focused ads. More importantly, Facebook is still learning how to get you to click on the ads it shows you. The rate of click-through on ads displayed on Facebook is lower than on Myspace and light years away from Google. To continue growing, Facebook needs to know what makes you click.

Beyond that, the philosophy that drives Facebook requires an ever-expanding base of information about every one of its users. The goal is to make your profile indistinguishable from your actual self, a core part of your identity in the same way as your voice or fingerprints. The more closely intertwined you are with your profile, the closer to the center of your entire web experience your profile becomes.

How many websites do you frequent that already allow you to connect with Facebook in some way, either by sharing their content on your page, liking their content, or permanently linking your behavior on their site to your Facebook profile? Those linkages do more than allow Facebook and its partners to share your private information. They make Facebook the beginning and end of every trip you take on the Information Superhighway.

WHY SHOULD YOU BE WORRIED ABOUT IT?

Facebook boasts revenue of only about $800 million a year, but could be worth as much as $15 billion. Though the company only turned cash-flow positive in 2009, its vast net worth and host of big-money investors make it extremely unlikely that anything short of the sudden death of a hundred million users could threaten its survival. Still, Facebook is going to do everything it can to avoid damage to its bottom line.

Facebook's bread is buttered with your tasty personal details. For all intents and purposes, any content you add to Facebook is owned by Facebook, and therefore becomes a commodity in its extraordinarily deep portfolio of psychographic data. Facebook will use that information any way it can to make money. It's a corporation, and its purpose is to make money.

Any paranoiac worth his tinfoil hat worries first and foremost about the government: What they know; what they think they know; what they do with all those black helicopters. Facebook, as a young company with ambitions of world conquest, wants very badly not to annoy the government, so it goes out of its way to be accommodating.

With the aid of Facebook, the government could know quite a lot about you. Government spooks might be friending you under false names, trolling your pictures and status updates for any hint of illegal activity. Even more alarming, however, is a Justice Department document that mentions Facebook is "often cooperative with emergency requests."

That means that when the feds approach Facebook asking for information, the company is likely to surrender it—with or without a warrant—as long as the government promises it's really, really important. But then, why worry? If you can't trust the government with private information obtained secretly, who can you trust?

Also—and here's a fun thought—Facebook is an American company, but it operates globally. If it's willing to surrender information about users to the U.S. Justice Department, why would it be unwilling to surrender similar information to other governments?

Interestingly, Facebook has become a critical resource for human rights activists around the globe. Facebook (and Twitter, YouTube, and other similar sites) was critical in organizing and raising the profile of the Green Revolution in Iran. It was a two-way street: The open nature of the site made identifying protesters relatively simple for the government; however, thanks to the speed of the social network, the government couldn't stop the video of the brutal killing of Neda Agha-Soltan from being posted and propagated. The Iranian government was reduced to complaining (and then following up with mass arrests and torture).

It's important to note that Facebook didn't take much of an active role in this drama. The network was a tool of both empowerment and repression. The Iranian secret police clearly fear the power of social networking sites, going so far as to question foreign visitors about their accounts.

Suing for privacy

What Facebook actually does with the information you provide can be very hard to determine. For years, Facebook's privacy policy has been a moving target, with updates and changes sometimes occurring every few months. A series of initiatives—including the program Beacon, which shared your behavior on third-party sites with Facebook—launched with no choice to opt-out, or with confusing or hidden configuration options.

The history of Facebook is a morass of criticisms and lawsuits over privacy issues and intellectual property. Some corporations and countries have banned the site as a security risk, while others use it to spy on their employees and citizens. A look into the history of the company, and the number of complaints that have been raised against it and some of its principal executives, should lead any reasonable person to have some serious ethical questions.

Actual statistics are tough to come by, but by all accounts, criminals flock to Facebook and other social networks. Blackmail, murder, suicide, confidence games, false representation, stalking, bullying—all of these things can and do happen. When you open yourself up online, someone will always be waiting to punish you for it, either by taking advantage of you or psychologically brutalizing you.

WHAT CAN YOU DO ABOUT IT?

Abstinence makes you stronger

As with herpes, once you've got a Facebook profile, you're pretty much stuck with it. Even if you delete your profile, your information could be saved on the Facebook servers for up to six months. Any photos of you that live in other people's albums will remain, tagged with your name. Comments you've made on other walls will live on forever.

The only sure way to protect yourself is total abstinence. Don't sign up, and the risk you run is minimized. If you've got friends with profiles, ask them very politely to crop you out of any photos they plan to post, or at the very least not to tag you by name.

If you've already got a Facebook account, making moves now to protect yourself may be futile, but there are some steps you can take to limit your exposure and guard at least some of your personal information.

Pick your friends

Eliminate people you don't know from your friends list. Strike the people you don't like. Do away with those you don't trust. Don't be sucked into the idea that more friends are somehow better. The fewer friends you have, the less information Facebook has about you, and the slimmer your chances of handing off sensitive information to someone you don't trust. When you create events, send them to private and select attendees. Be as judicious about who you associate with online as you are in real life.

Make yourself exclusive

In the Account tab on your Facebook profile, you can set almost every part of your profile to be viewable only to your friends. You cannot specify which friends can see what information, but if you've picked your friends carefully, that shouldn't matter. Think about the information you're offering through your profile and your status updates and decide who you actually want to know it.

Most of the settings you can manipulate are pretty innocuous, but hidden among the other settings is something that Facebook doesn't tell you about when you sign up. It's the sort of thing that wouldn't even occur to most websites, because the violation of privacy is so blatant and obvious it's startling.

Click on the Applications, Games and Websites button in your privacy settings. On that page, there's an "Info accessible through friends" section. See, when your friends play a game or use an application on Facebook, that application can see not only your friend's profiles, but yours as well. Whether you play or not, Farmville has access, through your friends, to your relationship status, religious views, and all of your photos. Go ahead and uncheck every single box on that page.

Likewise, disable Instant Personalization and Public Search to limit the amount of information Facebook shares with third parties.

With all of that done, you're still a celebrity, and Facebook is still a crowd of paparazzi parked on your lawn, but at least you've managed to pull the shades before you do anything embarrassing.

Publish wisely

Underneath your status update window, there's a little arrow. Click on that, and Facebook lets you decide who gets to read your status update and who it's hidden from. It's great for planning surprise parties and insulting people behind their backs. You can even set a new default for all of your status updates going forward.

Also—and this applies double to everyone under eighteen—before you post something, think about it for a few seconds. Maybe write it down on a little piece of paper and look at it before you even type it into the status update window. Try pinning it to the wall, and imagine it hanging outside the door to your office or dorm room. Would you hang it up there? Are you sure you want everyone in the world to hear what you're about to say? Do your parents and employers need to know whatever it is you have to declare about boobs, weed, Four Loko, and/or throwing up? Does the person you're about to insult have access to your feed (because as subtle as you think you're being—you're not)? Let's all try working together to raise the level of discourse here by just considering, for five seconds, what we've typed before we hit that "Update" button.

CHAPTER 3

SUPER SAVER OR HIGH-TECH SCAM? GROCERY STORE DISCOUNT CARDS

You like saving money. Who doesn't? Money is awesome, but what are you giving away for the thirty-two cents you just saved on Skippy?

THREAT LEVEL

WHAT IS IT?

If you shop at any major grocery store chain, you've probably got one. Your key chain might even be crowded with them—two for the grocery stores you usually shop at, one for the drug store that services your prescriptions, another for the place you buy cat food . . . . They are your local shop's reward to you for being such a loyal customer.

You hunt hungrily for the telltale yellow tags that mean savings. You fill your shopping cart with marked-down items and head home feeling smug about scamming the store out of thirty cents on the dollar. It is a deeply satisfying way to shop—a fact the grocery chains rely on to keep you using their discount cards.

As with so many of the little pleasures in life, the savings offered by discount cards are largely an illusion. Whether you use one or not, shopping at a grocery store running a discount card program probably costs you more money, not to mention some of your privacy. Somewhere, there is a database with a log of every purchase you've made using your card. It's embarrassing enough to cruise through a checkout lane with nothing but Spam and macaroni and cheese in your cart; do you really want anyone to know how often you do that?

HOW DOES IT WORK?

Each discount card includes a unique bar code. When you signed up for the program, you gave your name and probably your address and phone number as well. That information is mated to your card in the store's computer.

Throughout the market are discounts you only receive if you scan your card at the check stand. The savings on these items often seem extreme, with buy-one-get-one offers and discounts of 50 percent and more being common. The sensation of savings is palpable.

How does the store afford to give you such great deals? For large chains, a program like this costs as much as $30 million to start, with annual maintenance costing $5–$10 million. Safeway in the United Kingdom spent up to $70 million a year on their program. Such a vast amount of money exceeds by far the scope of thanking customers for their loyalty. So why do it?

The answer, of course, is that the store jacks up its prices across the board. Those consumers not taking part in the discount program foot the bulk of the bill. Even if you have the discount card, the store inflates the nondiscounted items you inevitably buy. You're spending about as much now as you would have before the store implemented the program.

From prescriptions to pumpernickel, the check stand logs every purchase you make and associates it with the bar code on the back of your card. You would think that the store would use this information to target you for direct-mail marketing in the same way that websites use similar information for ad targeting, but that's not the case. Most stores have privacy policies that don't allow them to use your information in that manner.

The real reason the store tracks your shopping is that it allows the company to identify who their highest value shoppers are—the 20 percent or so of people who spend the most. Stores use that information to modify their product selection. If the top 20 percent of shoppers buy a lot of chips and not much chili, look for the chips section to expand and the chili selection to decrease, even if the other 80 percent of consumers love chili. Over time, product selection in general will narrow. You will find yourself shopping in a store with whole aisles you never enter, full of deeply discounted items targeted at the big spenders. Even with the discount card, the prices you pay are slightly higher than the prices paid by that upper tier of shoppers. Those poor bastards who don't take part in the program pay through the nose to support the chip-obsessed moneybags in the top fifth.

You can already see this in effect. Keep an eye out around Thanksgiving. Does your supermarket offer free turkeys to people who spend enough money? Did you get one? If so, congratulations! You're in the top 20 percent. If you ended up buying your own turkey, chances are it was marked up a few cents to pay for the free bird next door. Happy Thanksgiving.

WHO INVENTED IT AND WHY?

The concept was inspired by frequent flier programs, the first of which was launched by Texas International Airlines in 1979. Other airlines soon followed, and now it's difficult to imagine air travel without frequent flier programs.

It's tough to say what grocery chain introduced the first discount card, but by the mid-nineties they were ubiquitous and had expanded well beyond the supermarket. Gas stations, drug stores, record shops, and pet supply chains all launched similar programs.

This was done because retailers wanted to know more about you. Before discount card programs existed, the only way your local supermarket had of communicating with you was to simply hurl advertising and hope it stuck. They could track the general behavior of their customers, but they couldn't drill down into that data. They knew people bought a lot of steak and a lot of Cool Whip, but was it the same people buying both? An ad selling steak and Cool Whip together could really entice people, or it could just gross everyone out.

Discount card programs give retailers specific, individual data about the shopping habits of their customers. Shopper profiles and correlations between products can be built based on purchasing history. Before the discount card programs, supermarkets knew about us as a group. Now they know about you as an individual.

WHO'S USING IT TO WATCH YOU?

No one you really need to be afraid of—yet

The only people using these programs to keep an eye on you are the supermarkets. They don't share the information (except with their market-research firms), they don't mine it for personally identifying intelligence, and they don't target you for direct-mail programs or phone calls (yet). They don't even care if you use your real name and address when you sign up.

All they care about is your shopper profile. They want to know what you eat, what you drink, what kind of drugs you use when you get sick, how often you blow your nose, and how much toilet paper you go through in a week. And, of course, what they really care about is how much money you spend. The more you buy, the more they care.

WHY IS IT WATCHING YOU?

The logic behind the original frequent flier program was that customers, given the opportunity to earn something free, would return over and over again to the same airline. It's extremely rare that an airport is served by only a single airline, and air travel in general is an optional expense, so it is difficult for airlines to take advantage of the information gathered by their rewards programs. Targeting only specific slices of the frequent flier membership would be counterproductive, driving previously dedicated customers into the arms of competitors.

The difference between frequent flier programs and supermarket discount cards is that people need what's sold in supermarkets to live—or at least to maintain a certain quality of life. In some markets, there is little or no competition, with only a single grocery store available. In these cases, it is very easy for a store to play favorites with the most profitable slice of the population.

The purpose of a discount card program is to minimize effort and maximize profit through meaningful targeting of product selection. A store can make more money selling a specific selection of products to the richest 20 percent of the people in your town rather than providing a general selection to everyone. The supermarket watches you for the same reason any other business does—because it is profitable to do so.

WHY SHOULD YOU BE WORRIED ABOUT IT?

Even in locations with multiple supermarkets, that top 20 percent is going to be the same group of people at every store. If you're not in that 20 percent—and the magic of math says you probably aren't—you're going to pay more for an increasingly poorer selection no matter what you do.

Eventually, supermarkets will exhaust the possibilities of segmenting their market and will turn to new methods of using the information collected by their discount program. Look for a posted notification that the store's privacy policy has changed. Then keep an eye out for the direct mail and phone campaigns. Depending on what information you gave them when you signed up, they might know how many kids you have, your age, your marital status, and where you work. Even if you didn't volunteer that information, they can guess at a lot of it based on your purchase history. Imagine, if you will, a near future in which the phone rings just as you sit down to a nice steak dinner. It's the supermarket, wondering how you're enjoying that steak and suggesting that next time you might want to purchase some steak sauce to go along with it.

WHAT CAN YOU DO ABOUT IT?

Just say no

In most places, you have options other than the grocery chains. Shop somewhere that doesn't offer a discount program—it might feel like you're spending more, but if you keep track you'll probably find that you aren't. If you can afford it, join a Community Supported Agriculture organization and buy local. Patronize shops that don't think it's any of their business that you're buying nothing but cake frosting and a single plastic spoon.

Complain. It's fun!

If a supermarket with a discount program is your only option, encourage the management to discontinue the store's participation. It probably won't work, but corporations often respond to consumer complaints.

Volunteer!

You can join an organization like Consumers Against Supermarket Privacy Invasion and Numbering (C.A.S.P.I.A.N.), an organization dedicated specifically to combating invasive marketing and consumer tracking tactics. Their website (*www.nocards.org*) is full of scary information about market segmentation and RFID tracking.

RFID EMBEDDING— QUIT WEARING UNDERWEAR AND USING CREDIT CARDS BEFORE IT'S TOO LATE

They're smaller than a grain of sand, as unique as snowflakes, so cheap they might as well be free, and they are everywhere.

THREAT LEVEL

WHAT IS IT?

RFID (Radio Frequency Identification) tags are small computer chips attached to an antenna. When pinged by a reader device (also called an interrogator device, to make it sound scary), the RFID tag broadcasts whatever information it has been programmed with. This information can be as simple as a short string of numbers (like the numbers at the bottom of a bar code or a credit card number) or as complex as photos and packets of encrypted data.

The transmission range of an RFID chip is limited by the power source of the chip and the size of the antenna. The most common ones are thick labels with a strip of conductive material running like a maze around a tiny chip in the middle. If you bought this book at a major retailer or got it in a library, there might be one stuck to the inside cover. Check it out. I'll wait.

The smallest RFID chips are roughly the size of a speck of dust—small and light enough to float on the convection currents in a sunbeam like a cat hair. At such diminutive sizes, it is difficult to attach an antenna—limiting transmission range to only a few millimeters—and information storage is limited to a short string of numbers, but technology improves constantly.

Organizations from libraries to hospitals to armies to grocery stores use this technology for inventory tracking. The United States, European Union, and a number of other countries have embedded them in passports to ease immigration control. Cell phone manufacturers include programmable versions in their devices to allow you to link your phone to your bank account or credit cards. If you drive regularly on toll roads, you probably have one—in the form of a small plastic box—stuck to the inside of your windshield. You might have several in your wallet, masquerading as a workplace key card, library card, credit card, or subway fare card.

Many of these tags carry harmless data in the form of stored value without any personally identifying information—as in the case of your subway fare card or the FastPass in your car. But most of them carry at least some sensitive information. Every tag is unique, meaning that even the innocuous ones can be used to track you.

With the increasing ubiquity of RFID tags, each of us sacrifices more and more locational privacy. Soon our wallets, clothing, and key rings will be bursting with easily tracked radio signatures. The stores we shop at, the companies whose brands we buy, our employers, and our government will all be keeping an eye on our location and habits.

HOW DOES IT WORK?

The interrogator device sends out a signal looking for nearby tags. When a tag receives that signal, it transmits whatever information it has been programmed to transmit. Hand-held interrogators are used for things like inventory control—scanning items in and out of a warehouse, for instance. Stationary scanners exist for applications in which the tags themselves are highly mobile, like toll booths and passport control. Any interrogator can be used to track location—if you know where the interrogator is, you know where any tags it scans are.

There are three ways of powering the transmission sent by an RFID tag. Passive tags don't carry their own batteries, making them small and inexpensive. They borrow the power to send their data payload from incoming signals—meaning that when an interrogator sends a signal to the tag, leftover energy from the incoming signal powers the transmission. Range is limited by the amount of power put into the tag, but it can be more than sixty feet. Because they're cheap, passive tags are most common in consumer goods. They're also the least secure. It takes energy to encrypt information—low power means weak or nonexistent encryption.

Active RFID tags include batteries. They're bigger and more expensive than their passive cousins, capable of broadcasting farther, but also capable of stronger security. They actively try to get the attention of interrogators. When they find one, they can transmit more than 200 yards. If you've got one of these on you, that's a circle a fifth of a mile across, in which anyone could be receiving information and getting a rough idea of where you are. With multiple interrogators or the GPS unit that some active tags carry, your exact location becomes public knowledge.

The third kind of RFID tag is a battery-assisted passive tag. These are comparable in size to active tags, but they're less enthusiastic. They conserve their energy until they receive a query from an interrogator, then they broadcast their payload with a range similar to active tags.

By the time you read this, passive tags could be as cheap as one cent. Spending a single cent to include a tag on every product could translate to thousands or hundreds of thousands of dollars in assets and supply chain management savings for retailers and manufacturers. In the near future, everything you buy, from new cars to fun-size Kit Kats, will include an RFID tag.

Checked out when you check out

Most tags currently in use are meant to register a single item one time or track the movements of a high-value asset like a computer or a piece of military hardware. The tags pasted inside the covers of books at the library are scanned when a book is checked out and when it returns, largely eliminating human error from the library's inventory management. If you work at a large company, some of their laptops or other computer equipment might have active RFID tags attached to them, allowing the company to keep track of who has their equipment and where it is. If you've got an RFID-enabled phone, you can link it directly to your credit cards and—at retailers equipped with the proper interrogator— simply pick up an RFID-embedded item and walk out without ever visiting the cashier. If you don't have that kind of phone and just decide to walk out with a tube of Pringles, the retailer could know instantly that you've stolen something—and he could track you down.

More sophisticated tags can do more than just remember and transmit preprogrammed information. Active tags could know how much milk is left in a jug or how many pickles remain in a jar. They might talk directly to your new fridge, which could, in turn, transmit its contents to your local supermarket. Any perishable item could be smart enough to know when its time has come, and gossipy enough to tell a retailer. Walk into a store carrying an RFID-enabled credit card, and you could immediately be subjected to ads targeted directly at you; reminders that you're out of tampons, the milk has gone bad, and your kids need more Go-gurt.

Minispies are everywhere

In the name of convenience, corporations, marketers, and even your employer are sending tiny electronic spies directly into your home. They're embedding your clothing, your food, and your gadgets with tracking devices so that they can tailor their services to you. You are being turned into a beacon; a blip on a thousand retail radar screens, unable to hide and incapable of keeping your personal life personal.

RFID tags are all the rage among people who view the future as a bright and shining place where all information is free. In this future, people are happy to give up their privacy in order to shop without ever having to look another human being in the eye or, horror of horrors, actually interact in something as base as a cash transaction. But for the rest of us—who'd rather not have strangers tracking every purchase and mapping every move—they're the enemy.

WHO INVENTED IT AND WHY?

Ask a historian who invented radio, and you'll get a very long, boring story about one of the most contentious debates in the history of science. The origins of radio throng with big, nineteenth-century names like Bose, Hughes, Hertz, Marconi, and Tesla. (Who also invented a death ray. Seriously. Look it up.) Experiments with the transmission of electromagnetic signals were already being performed in the early 1800s. By the 1890s, what was then known as "wireless telegraphy" had become a focus of intense study and ruthless competition. By the early 1900s, radio was ubiquitous and hugely popular.

The precursor to the modern RFID chip was invented in Germany during World War II. Transponders that functioned very much like RFID technology were installed in airplanes on both sides of the war. Clunky, stupid (from a computing perspective), and easily vulnerable to operator error, they often gave away the location of air formations to enemy forces. But they also allowed much more organized use of air assets. During the Battle of Britain, the ability of the British to swiftly organize and deploy their forces saved lives and handed the Nazis their first major defeat.

In the sixties, a technology known as Electronic Article Surveillance was invented to deter shoplifting. This tech is still in use today. EAS tags are those awkward plastic things that jab you in the kidneys every time you try on a shirt. They operate by radio or magnetism and are the truest ancestor to the modern RFID.

Fast forward to 1970, when a man named Mario Cardullo filed a patent for the original RFID—what he called an Encoder. Even at the very beginning, Cardullo saw the potential of his invention—the original patent includes automated toll collection and inventory tracking as possible uses for the technology. Interestingly, when Cardullo and his team presented the idea to the New York Port Authority as an automated toll collection system, the Port Authority rep expressed concerns about the unconstitutional violation of privacy the technology enabled.

Within a few years, several companies had developed their own versions of Cardullo's Encoder. Despite the flurry of development, widespread adoption of the technology took almost twenty years; it wasn't until the nineties that RFID saw use for toll collection, and it's only now that the technology is being adapted to other uses.

WHO'S USING IT TO WATCH YOU?

The government

If you're a U.S. citizen and you've gotten a new passport in the last few years, guess what? There's an RFID chip in there. That alone isn't a big deal, since the passport itself is a method of tracking your movements. Government agents sit in airports all over the country, carefully logging the visas stamped in passports, asking invasive questions, and being generally nosy.

Now they don't need an actual physical presence to track you, and the capability to do so doesn't end when you're out of the visual range of the dude in the bulletproof booth. The tag inside your passport has a broadcast range of a little over thirty feet. The first batch of tagged passports included no shielding and no encryption. More recently, the government's added a thin metal sheet to the cover of the passport and weak encryption to the chip itself, but the effectiveness of these measures has yet to be established.

Everyone with something to sell

The government's hunger to know where you are and what you're doing pales in comparison to that of corporate America. The potential of the technology is vast. It could save or generate millions by enabling simpler shipment tracking and inventory control, creating new, innovative means of communicating directly with consumers, and spawning unheard-of concepts for customized user experiences.

RFID tagging in the consumer sphere is all about convenience. Imagine a world in which your shopping cart knows what products you place into it, updating you in real time with the amount you're spending, the calorie content of what you're buying, and maybe even recipe suggestions. The store is surprisingly quiet, because the check stands have been eliminated; you bag your groceries yourself and wheel your cart out the door. As soon as you pass the threshold, your credit card is automatically charged.

At home, your cupboards and refrigerator listen for new products. As you drink your orange juice and eat your eggs, the cartons keep your fridge up to date about their remaining contents. Your fridge reminds you when you're almost out, and updates the local grocery store so that your smart cart can remind you again as you wander through the aisles trying to remember that one last thing you forgot.

Every shop in the mall has this capability, eliminating human helpers in favor of retail space. Soft, mechanical voices greet you by name when you enter. Personalized music plays in the fitting room. Clothing racks make gentle suggestions about what you might like based on past purchases and where to find your size. Shoes tell you in advance whether they'll be comfortable or not. Video games and toys scream at you, claiming exciting new features never before seen by human eyes. Cell phones and cameras beep and wink as you walk by. Ads shift and shimmer, taking on forms based on what you've touched, what you've looked at, and what you've bought. Thanks to RFID, you are integrated seamlessly into your own private consumer experience, coddled and catered to and kept as satisfied as possible by 100 tiny machines all invisibly chattering back and forth.

Hospitals

The newest and best medical implants and prostheses feature RFID tags or other technology to allow your doctor to monitor your health and the performance of the device. Computer-controlled pacemakers, connected by RFID or Wi-Fi, can be adjusted without surgery. Prostheses embedded with an RFID tag can tell a doctor or manufacturer all they need to know about the patient in case a replacement or adjustment is needed. Subdermal chips give caregivers access to the medical history of an unconscious or uncommunicative patient. Of course, anyone else with an interrogator can gain access to your medical history and prescriptions.

Criminals and terrorists

RFID chips love to share what they know, and business and the government aren't the only folks listening. Home building an interrogator or RFID remote cloning device is simple and cheap. Imagine a wallet full of RFID-enabled credit cards. Unless your pocket is lined with copper mesh and welded shut, those credit cards are all broadcasting a radio signal that includes your name, your credit card number, and your address. You might as well walk around screaming your social security number at people. Most of that information is probably encrypted—but any crook savvy enough to build a machine for stealing your credit card information over the air probably has a computer rig at home beefy enough to snap the weak encryption on most RFID chips like a Slim Jim.

If you've got a newer car, the fancy key fob that lets you start your car without inserting a key into the ignition is equipped with RFID. Those tags can be cloned, and your car will never know the difference between you and the thief behind the wheel.

There's a thriving worldwide black market for stolen passports. Some go to refugees hoping to sneak into the United States or Europe in search of a better life; some go to the sorts of people who crash airplanes into buildings. Thanks to RFID, passport thieves don't need to lay a finger on you to get hold of your documents.

WHY IS IT WATCHING YOU?

RFID tagging is the next generation in safety and convenience. Tags expedite financial transactions, speed our way through passport control, and accelerate toll collection on the turnpike.

The government will tell you that RFID adds a layer of security to your identification. The tag in your passport (and soon to be in your driver's license) is like a digital fingerprint—a supplement to the picture and signature on the ID. Simply by adding a new layer of technical sophistication, passports become slightly more difficult to counterfeit. A stolen passport cannot simply be cut up and pasted back together to create a usable forgery.

Retailers and manufacturers want to know as much as they can about you. Most data available to marketers is aggregate—data generated by tracking entire populations. A marketer can predict with reasonable certainty what a group of seventeen-year-olds might do, but the behavior of an individual seventeen-year-old is just as opaque to the marketing director of American Eagle Outfitters as it is to the rest of us.

RFID makes profiling individual consumers cheap and easy. Marketers will track you as closely as possible, by any means at their disposal, because they want you to buy more of whatever it is they have to sell. If detergent companies could keep track of how dirty your clothes are, they would. If cosmetics companies could inject something into your skin to track its moisture level, they would. With RFID, they will soon be able to do these things and more.

The possibilities go way beyond what we currently think of as advertising. Given the ability to track your movements and record your spending, marketers can immerse you in a nonstop barrage of targeted marketing—an envelope of refined messaging made just for you. A walk through the mall could be an unbroken string of free offers, unbeatable deals, and seamless shopping. If you're not in the mood to be advertised to, that's just fine—that's useful data, too.

They're on to you

Businesses do not do these things to annoy you. They invade your life in order to tailor their products to you. Good products enhance your quality of life; it stands to reason that an experience customized just for you will maximize that effect.

Most businesses will restrain themselves, preferring to sell you a pleasant, personalized experience or product for which you will grow to feel genuine affection. But if your e-mail address has ever become overwhelmed with spam, you know that it takes very little effort to turn what might once have been fun into a nightmare slog. Your walk through the mall could suddenly shift from a pleasant, personalized experience to a broadside of unavoidable hard sells and porn assaults. The first time your underwear suggests natural male enhancement you'll see what I mean.

If the motivation of corporate America is ultimately profit—and it is—that goes double for the criminal element. Car theft, identity theft, big-ticket robbery . . . these are but a few of the possibilities made easier by RFID technology. Identity theft alone is a multibillion-dollar business, and the consequences to you could be anything from an empty bank account and a ruined credit rating to seeing your name in the newspaper under the picture of a mass murderer.

WHY SHOULD YOU BE WORRIED ABOUT IT?

RFID technology has huge potential to enhance our safety and increase our convenience, but at what cost? In the name of easier shopping, we could allow ourselves to become a blip on 1,000 radar screens—a trackable asset rather than a person. It's up to you how much you're willing to give up to get in and out of the mall faster.

The signal broadcast by an RFID tag is a burst, scattering signal in every direction. Any receiver within a few inches to hundreds of feet could be picking up your location or other information. Interrogators can be as small as a wallet and cost less than $200 to build.

A criminal with a cloning device could brush against you and instantly gain access to your workplace, your vehicle, your credit cards, and your passport information. From there, he could steal your identity and rob you blind, clear out your office and let you take the blame, and drive away in your car without setting off the alarm.

The potential for government abuse of RFID tags is vast. Like any organization concerned with the acquisition and retention of power, governments are vulnerable to temptation. Given the ability to easily track where you shop, what books you borrow from the library, whom you talk to, and where you go, few governments would be able to resist. To be able to track everyone, all the time, on the off chance that one person in a thousand is dangerous—this is the ideal of any internal security organization, no matter how benign.

Tracking your Euros

Some governments are already beginning to give in to this temptation. The European Union may have already begun experimenting with implanting RFID tags in their currency. If the EU succeeds in implementing this, can the United States be far behind? Cash has long been the mainstay of people who wish to perform anonymous financial transactions. The basis of the American economy—and by extension, the economy of the entire world—is the free flow of capital. To rob cash transactions of anonymity is to end that free flow and possibly discourage the use of cash.

Even if you want to eliminate RFID tags from your life, it's unlikely you'll be able to. They are small and getting smaller. They can be woven into clothing, embedded in paper, or injected under your skin. Finding them is already difficult, and extracting them from the products into which they are embedded can be even harder.

Whether you are the target of a malicious government, a greedy corporation, or a hardened criminal, RFID tags will be impossible to avoid. Within a couple of years, all of us will be broadcasting our own private radio show.

WHAT CAN YOU DO ABOUT IT?

Kill the bug

There are a few ways you can kill RFID tags. Not all of them are foolproof, or even safe. Some of them may destroy the product in which the tag is embedded.

If safety is of little concern, the easiest and fastest way to murder these little spies is to cook them. Throw any RFID-embedded item in the microwave for three to five seconds. This will destroy the antenna and probably melt the chip. Be aware that doing this involves a fire risk, and will almost certainly scorch whatever item you've decided to nuke. Your passport will be destroyed, your credit card will be rendered useless, and your underwear may burst into flames. A small price to pay for privacy.

If you can find the chip, you can also physically maul it, either by smashing it with a hammer or stabbing it (an X-acto knife or straight pin works best). If you're trying to cripple the tag in your passport, stabbing it is a bad idea—passports that bear evidence of physical damage or tampering are no longer legal forms of ID. So think carefully before you get drunk and go after your passport with a carving knife.

The hammer method is best for passports and driver's licenses. Wrap the ID in a thin towel to avoid leaving big, obvious circles on its face and give it a few solid whacks. Passports without functional tags are still legally acceptable, though you may incur an odd look or a few extra questions from the passport control officer. Avoid the temptation to brag about what you've done.

Cut it out

Since you've already got the X-acto knife out, there's another physically aggressive method for slaughtering RFID tags. If you look at a tag, the chip itself will be a small rectangle, usually near the center of a coil of wire (the antenna). The connection points between the chip and the antenna should be fairly obvious. Cut those connections and the chip will be unable to broadcast or receive.

If you want to play it extra safe, cut the chip entirely out of the tag. Flush it down the toilet to show your contempt.

Block the signal

It's fairly simple to block most RFID tags. There are RFID-blocking wallets and passport holders available online, or you can build a little portable Faraday cage for your pocket.

To build your own RFID-blocking gear, you will need to build a pocketbook out of copper or aluminum sheets. This has the added benefit of making you look awesome—especially if you use copper and fashion it into a steampunk lunchbox.

There is some evidence that your body itself is a reasonably effective shielding device. Keep your passport and other RFID-enabled items inside your clothes against your skin. That might, at least, limit the number of directions from which you can be tracked.

Outsmart the bug

Feeling confident? Good. This one's for you then.

Interrogator devices are reasonably cheap and can be purchased legally. For people with a little bit of programming experience, they are relatively simple to use. With an interrogator/programmer, you can hack into any RFID chip about which you're concerned and erase the information on it. Tags can't tell what they don't know.

Demand secrecy

If your employer asks you to use a tagged ID card, ask him or her what level of encryption they've included. If the security chief of your company just stares at you, that means there's no encryption on your ID. That's not surprising. Encryption is expensive and energy-intensive and may just not be cost-effective when it comes to distributing key cards to dozens or hundreds of employees. Politely point out that a kid with a $150 cloner in the parking lot could steal a VP's identification and rob the company blind. After that, you'll probably want to meekly accept the ID card and put it in your RFID-blocking wallet. You can't force your company to do anything, but you can at least control access to the information contained in your own pocket.

Credit card companies are a different matter. They probably do include some encryption on their cards. More than likely it will be a challenge-response system (like a password) or an encryption algorithm the company developed in-house. Both types of protection are what is known as "pointless"—the challenge-response because it is vulnerable to a brute force attack (in which a computer randomly tries different key combinations until one works), and the in-house algorithm because it is not extensively tested and therefore could be broken at any moment. If company reps start giving you numbers like 128-bit or 150-bit, stop them and ask for the name of the algorithm. Look it up online. If you find a blog by a guy with a name like cr3d!td3^1l bragging about how he 0wnZ0r3ed that algorithm, throw your credit card into the first volcano you can find.

Demand that your credit card company switch to a tested strong encryption like PGP or the National Security Agency's SHA-1 or SHA-2. Cut up the card they've given you (or just stab the chip in it with an icepick) and demand they send you a new one that's actually immune to identity theft. If they refuse, cancel your account and go with a credit card company that's interested in protecting its clients.

CHAPTER 5

POCKET-SIZED SPIES—HOW YOUR GADGETS BETRAY YOU

You love your gadgets. You've got a ton of them. You carry all of them on your belt because some small part of you imagines you wear a mask and cape and fight criminals like the Joker and the Penguin.

You are not Batman. You are a target.

THREAT LEVEL

WHAT IS IT?

If you own a popular device that connects to the Internet, some-one, somewhere, is trying to track it, break it, or steal it.

The issue is complexity. Complexity also means vulnerabil-ity. The more complex a device becomes, the more difficult and expensive it is to protect. To keep smartphones and other high-tech devices affordable, their manufacturers do the absolute minimum to protect them from hackers and other malicious individuals.

Companies do their best to minimize or hide vulnerabilities, but bulletproof software and hardware are for military applications where price is no object. For consumer products, engineers are lim-ited by cost. Budget always has the final say, and most Internet-capable devices hit the market accompanied by prayers that hackers never notice the back doors that have been left in place.

It's the Wild West on the Internet, complete with folks who will shoot you just to watch you die. The black hat community (hack-ers who specialize in network intrusion and computer viruses) will target anything that becomes popular, probe it for weaknesses, and destroy, if possible. They don't do this because they're bastards; some black hats claim to be performing a service, arguing that if they discover and exploit a weakness, it teaches The Man a lesson about security. Most of us, noticing a serious flaw in a security setup, would write a letter. Black hats figure writing letters is for wimps. A much more effective way to point out a security flaw, they feel, is to write a virus that brings down air traffic control or fries a nuclear power plant. It sounds totally reasonable if you're a douche.

Hackers aren't the only people you need to worry about. Anything you own that connects to the Internet, contains a GPS, or otherwise receives a signal can be tracked. Even without all the RFID tags in our clothes, without the frequent-shopper cards and IP logging and consumer profiling, we walk around like digital rabbits leaving a trail of little electronic poops. Anyone with the proper tools can follow us.

HOW DOES IT WORK?

Most of your toys require an Internet connection to update their software. This is an ideal vector for hackers to attack you. Malicious software, secretly installed on your home computer, could easily load itself into your mobile device the next time you plug it in for an update. Your phone or GPS could be secretly converted into a spy that tells some shadowy third party everything he could ever need to know to steal your identity.

The GPS packed into your smartphone, installed in your dashboard, or mounted on your windshield keeps track of your location by using you as the pinnacle of an upside-down pyramid with three or four satellites forming the corners at the "base." The more satellites there are keeping track of you, the more accurate the GPS signal is, down to about ten feet. If you've got GPS, you probably don't even remember how you got anywhere without it.

You have vague memories of printing out maps from the Internet or—horror of horrors—getting bizarre directions over the phone from your stupidest friends. But this must be the product of a fever-driven nightmare.

When you're in an unfamiliar city, GPS is worth its weight in gold, but that convenience is a two-way street. In order to supply you with maps and directions, the system must be aware of your position. Consumer GPS signal is almost never encrypted. If your GPS system is turned on, whether you're using it or not, someone else could be using it to track you.

That's only the easiest and most obvious way to track you. Cellular networks are a rough grid of interlocking hexagons or circles with a cell tower at the center of each. Because the cells interlock and overlap, you can move from the coverage of one tower to the coverage of another without interruption in your service. This also allows cell towers to triangulate your position. When your phone is turned on, it communicates constantly with any nearby cell towers. If a government agency has locked onto your phone, they will always be able to determine your position, within 150 feet or so—accurate enough for a sniper to find you. Any device that connects to a cell network or wirelessly to the Internet can be tracked like this. The only thing that varies is the distance at which the tracking can be performed and the accuracy of the location.

WHO INVENTED IT AND WHY?

No one invented hacking—it's human nature. For as long as technology has existed, there have been people who wanted to take it apart, reverse engineer it, and break it. Those broken stone tools left by cavemen? Probably right after some clever caveman invented a tool, some other assclown caveman started coming up with ways to break it. If anyone ever hands you an ax or a sledgehammer, you immediately start looking around for something to chop into pieces or smash.

The Global Positioning System satellite network grew out of a five-satellite navigation system launched by the U.S. Navy in 1960. It has since grown into a network of more than two dozen satellites, open to use by anyone in the world.

The utility of mobile telephones was established back in World War II, with the use of radiotelephones by troops in the field. Large-scale commercial deployment of gigantic radiotelephones was impractical. Routing traffic without interference was complex enough to give telecommunications engineers aneurysms, and the power requirements of the gadgets made them viciously heavy. Building a network of transmission towers was the most elegant practical solution—allowing mobile phones to be miniaturized microwave transmitters rather than gigantic shortwave broadcasters.

The first cellular network was built in Japan in the early eighties, by Nippon Telegraph and Telephone. If you do a Google image search, you can find thirty-year-old photos of Japanese businessmen hauling large, two-wheeled contraptions behind them. You might think those are rickshaws, but they're not. They're old cell phones.

WHO'S USING IT TO WATCH YOU?

Evil hackers

Hackers come in a million different flavors. Organized crime syndicates run vast computer scams geared for everything from software piracy to identity theft to bank fraud. Governments all over the world run clandestine networks that script and test cyber-warfare software on civilians. Online anarchists write viruses to damage or destroy large corporations. Individual black hats some-times do malicious things just because they're jerks.

The government—again

The government can't get enough of you. You're like Thursday night on NBC for the government. They'll keep watching you, even when you're in reruns, because they love you that much.

WHY IS IT WATCHING YOU?

The motivation for software hacking can be anything from pure malicious joy to criminal financial gain. Hacked phones and computers can be used for elaborate pranks, anarchic assaults, or destructive vendettas. They can also be used to capture sensitive financial information, passwords, or to steal your identity.

Millions of identity records are stolen every year. Your iden-tity could have been compromised months or years ago, and you might never know—or you might find out five years from now when some Russian mobster finally gets around to starting an Xbox Live account with it. Even if your ID or financial information never gets used, they are still valuable. Identities are traded on the black market just like guns and drugs. Your identity is a commodity, and criminals will gain access to it however they can.

The government probably isn't watching you, unless your cell phone was used as part of a crime. The police have to have prob-able cause and a warrant before they can tap and track a cell phone or a GPS unit. Federal agencies don't always pay attention to the law, but they are supposed to operate under the same constraints as the police. In any case, tracking every gadget in the world simply isn't possible. If the government is watching you through your mobile phone, it's doing so because you have valuable intelligence or information that can be used in a criminal prosecution.

WHY SHOULD YOU BE WORRIED ABOUT IT?

If you're a normal person, you are probably a thief. Millions of people use BitTorrent or other peer-to-peer utilities to illicitly acquire music or movies. Illegal downloads are a great way to distribute malicious software—hide a virus in a popular piece of content, and thousands or millions of people could infect their own computers.

A hacker interested in more than just burning your hard drive or turning your computer into a spam-distributing slave can trick you into installing software that will invade your phone or GPS. Once your device is infected, hackers gain access to your contacts list, your e-mail, your text messages, and your Internet traffic. They can log passwords and credit card numbers directly off your phone, and you might never suspect a thing.

Identity theft is an international industry worth billions. Because the link between the theft of personal information and actual fraud is often difficult to discern, no one can say for sure how bad the problem actually is, or even what your chances of being a victim are. What we do know, though, is that the potential gains for a criminal are huge, for a relatively small risk.

On the other side of the coin, a government with the ability to track every one of its citizens is a dangerous creature. A government that holds such a power will inevitably try to use it. The ability to track our movement is only a short step from the ability to control our movement, at which point the government becomes our owner rather than our servant.

WHAT CAN YOU DO ABOUT IT?

Power down

Turn your wireless devices off when you're not using them. If your gadgets are turned off, they can't talk to satellites or cell towers. If they can't talk, they can't be tracked. The less time you spend connected, the safer you are.

Downgrade

The less sophisticated your devices are, the less likely they are to be tracked or compromised. Ditch the high-end gadgets in favor of toys a few years old. Buy a digital camera without an always-on Wi-Fi connection. Trade in the Droid for an old flip phone. Sell your iPod Touch and buy yourself a six-year-old Zune. Throw away your GPS and print out Google maps at home. You still might be vulnerable to cell-tower triangulation, but you'll have eliminated a lot of connectivity and complexity, thereby reducing your vulnerability. If the government does try to find your phone using cell towers, they will see how little you have in the way of interesting tech, assume you're broke and/or deeply boring, and promptly go back to ignoring you.

Burn it

If you want to get real serious, get rid of the GPS, the smartphone, and all of the other conspicuous consumables. Buy yourself a supply of prepaid wireless phones (use cash!). Keep them turned off until you want to make a call, and never use the same phone more than once or twice. When you're done with them, burn or smash them to make sure they're destroyed.

Quit stealing

You can minimize the risk that your computer or mobile device will be compromised by malicious software by not stealing movies, music, and software. Stay off the torrent sites, buy your music legally, and pay a fair market value for software on physical media or through a reliable online source.

I know it's hard to pay for everything, and sometimes stealing is the only way to catch that episode of *Two and a Half Men* you missed, but you're going to have to deal with it. Illegal peer-to-peer transactions and sketchy websites are ideal ways to deliver bad bugs to your machine. If you want to truly protect yourself, you'll have to give them up.

This goes double for content of a more adult nature. Porn traffic is extremely high paced and anonymous, and users of adult torrent sites are less than happy about having to admit they've got a virus and where they picked it up. The sheer volume of content makes it impossible for the operators of a site to ensure its safety, and their motivation for doing so is pretty minimal. So pay for your porn! Those people work really hard. They deserve your money.

Use protection

Install a well-regarded antivirus suite on your computer. Pay the premium to enable all of the identity protection devices included in the software. Automate your virus scanner to run at least once a week—more if you spend a lot of time on unusual websites or can't give up your addiction to Russian mp3 sites. Antivirus programs aren't infallible, but they can go a long way toward protecting you.

PART II

THE GOVERNMENT IS WATCHING YOU

Even the friendliest, most benign government in the world likes to keep an eye on its citizens—it's a safe bet Canada has a few cameras posted around the country, just to make sure everyone's got enough poutine and warm clothing and that the moose don't get out of hand.

The excuse for this surveillance is always the same: The government watches you because it wants to keep you safe. If it knows where you are, what you're doing, and whom you're doing it with, it can protect you. If you've done nothing wrong, then you've got nothing to hide. Sacrifice a small amount of privacy, and we will keep you safe and warm, insulated from a dangerous world full of people who want to destroy our way of life—people we have, incidentally, under the exact same kind of surveillance.

Only a couple of decades ago the most popular method of spying on a population was to pay civilians to watch each other. That technique is still popular. When you see a sign offering a reward for information leading to an arrest, this is a solicitation to become a spy for the government. Do it enough, and they might even put missile launchers behind your car's headlights.

Nazi Germany, the Soviet Union, and North Korea relied (or rely, in the case of the glorious Democratic People's Republic of Korea) on vast human-intelligence organizations. Networks of hundreds or thousands or even hundreds of thousands (it has been estimated that one in four Soviet citizens worked for the KGB) of individuals spied on everyone they could. Recruiting spies and informers through blackmail, bribery, or threat, these nations relied on their own citizens to tattle on each other. They controlled access to information through the media, kept meticulous records, and used their networks of informants to destroy anyone who threatened the powers that be.

As technology has improved, the methods governments employ to watch people (and each other) have become more sophisticated, and less reliant on amateur snitches. Satellites hover above us with cameras powerful enough to detect whether we've cleaned our fingernails lately. Lasers listen in on our conversations. Sophisticated computers read our e-mail and listen to our phone calls. Tiny flakes of skin or strands of hair betray us through chemical tests that can unlock our genetics in a matter of minutes. Robots armed with missiles watch us from miles away, waiting for a target lock.

It all comes down to power. Powerful people live in terror of losing their status. Whether they're dictators or senators, they will do anything they can to remain where they are, or to climb higher. The temptation to watch people—to know their moods, to hear what they say about you—is overwhelming, and increases in proportion to the power they gain. Governments watch their citizens because they are afraid of the power an angry constituency can wield, either through force of arms or the weight of popular dissent.

Ironically, these days it is the democratic nations of the West that spend the most time and money—and employ the most fantastic technology—watching their citizens. They use the same excuses as the dictatorships of the last century, employ many of the same tactics, and often achieve similar results. Thanks to modern technology, they've got teams of robots hiding quietly in corners, watching us twenty-four hours a day, and reporting everything they see.

The people of the United States and the United Kingdom rank alongside the citizens of Russia and China as the most closely surveilled folks in the world. Get used to the idea. If the government decides to put you under the microscope, there's nothing you can do about it but smile and hope they don't notice the bag of weed in your underwear drawer.

CHAPTER 6

ECHELON—THE MONSTROUSLY HUGE GIANT SCARY GLOBAL SURVEILLANCE PROGRAM

It reads your e-mail, listens to your phone calls, and remembers everything you say. It is huge and unstoppable and it is always listening.

THREAT LEVEL

WHAT IS IT?

ECHELON (not an acronym—just written in all caps to make it scary) is the modern name for the largest and oldest signals intelligence-gathering operation in the world. Rumored to have been in development since 1947, and probably in operation since the late sixties, it operates under the auspices of an agreement signed by the world's five major English-speaking nations—the United States, the United Kingdom, Canada, Australia, and New Zealand, aka AUSCANNZUKUS (now *that's* an acronym).

In World War I, battles were won or lost by maneuvers planned before the first shot was ever fired—you transmitted orders by screaming as loud as you could. If the enemy outmaneuvered you, there was no way to react before your position was overrun and your men killed or captured. Human intelligence was king back then. Coded messages were handwritten using simple ciphers that today's BlackBerry could crack. Capturing these messages came down to identifying a courier and interrogating, torturing, or killing him. The codebreakers of the era were nowhere near as important as the agents in the field.

That all changed during the Second World War. In World War II, thousands of troops could be redeployed with a single radio command, air power and artillery could be directed to where the enemy was most concentrated, and endangered troops could call for help. The battlefield went from a static pit of mud and blood to the fluid chaos of modern war.

Signals intelligence (the practice of intercepting transmissions; it is distinct from human intelligence, which is the practice of putting people in a dark hole and hitting them with a bar of soap in a sock) became critical. Both sides of the war poured resources into encryption and code-breaking techniques, each hoping for an edge. It was the Allied command of signal interception and codebreaking that allowed them to give the Nazis the righteous ball stomping they so richly deserved.

Turing kicks butt

The Germans had dozens of genius mathematicians on their side, but the British had a guy named Alan Turing. Turing was such a badass math genius that he could solve complex differential equations just by pelvic thrusting and saying, "Boo-yah!" German code was so afraid of him it broke itself. Thanks to the work of Turing and his team, signals intelligence became indispensable. With a shortwave radio and a team of math nerds, you could sit comfortably at home (or, in the case of Turing, at the decoding center in Bletchley Park) and listen to the enemy tell you what he was going to do. The days of sending borderline psychopaths onto foreign soil to engage in mayhem were over.

Building something like ECHELON was a no-brainer. In the forties, we knew exactly where all the bad guys were—in Central Europe and Japan. After the war, we turned our attention to the countries behind the Iron Curtain. Why not build a worldwide listening organization designed to sift through every piece of information it could grab out of the air?

ECHELON is a worldwide network of satellite intercept stations, telephone network listening installations, and analytic computer systems scanning all the communications traffic it can for key words, trigger phrases, coded messages, and encrypted data. When it first began operation, it collected and sorted all of the signals intelligence coming out of the Soviet bloc; now it allows the English–speaking world's spooks to check out what's going on everywhere all the time.

Any time the National Security Agency is connected with a program like this, you know it's going to be trouble. The NSA is the favorite bogeyman of conspiracy theorists around the world—and with good reason. If the United States were going to create an organization specifically to employ evil supergeniuses, it would be the NSA. The CIA is full of smarter-than-average jocks that split their time between going over other people's bank statements and flying to foreign countries to kill people. The NSA is full of retired mathletes with a mean streak. ECHELON is the biggest toy in its toybox.

When the Soviet Union fell apart and everyone realized that the prospect of war with China was silly, the NSA was left with a giant ear and no bad guys to listen to. Or rather, the bad guys had scattered. Instead of gathering together conveniently in the same country, they disappeared into deserts and cities, hiding among the civilians of friendly nations. These days, the bad guys are everywhere.

ECHELON listens to everything it can, parses what it hears for references to drugs or terrorism, and lets your local black helicopter dispatcher know. Theoretically, that's all it does. But then, about ten years ago, an investigation by the European Parliament determined that ECHELON could be used for industrial espionage— meaning that the NSA, when it picks up a hint of an interesting innovation in Europe, might be passing along technical or strategic details to American businesses. If that's the case, what else are they listening for?

HOW DOES IT WORK?

Radio and satellite communications are easy to intercept, as long as you have billions of dollars to spend doing it and the space to spread out. With sites in Australia, New Zealand, the United Kingdom, the United States, Japan, and elsewhere, ECHELON has the world covered.

Radio is a stupid way to broadcast secure communications, even if you use code. When you use a radio, it squirts the signal in pretty much every direction for hundreds of miles. Anyone with an antenna can hear it. At the beginning of the Cold War, most military communication was done over shortwave radio, so the NSA just built antennas in a circle around the Soviet Union and hired a bunch of Russian-speaking analysts to sit there and listen. That was the beginning of ECHELON.

Telephone networks were likewise unsophisticated. Every telephone was connected to a central switching station that routed all traffic. Tap into one part of the network and you had access to the entire thing. The United States was really fond of tapping Soviet telephone networks—even going so far as to send submarines into Russian harbors to deploy divers to install taps on underwater cables. Submarines actually had self-destruct buttons in case they got caught doing this stuff.

When the world began switching over to satellite-based communications, ECHELON evolved. The microwave transmissions used in satellite networks are harder to intercept than radio. Still, microwave scatters enough that you can capture the signal as long as you have a big enough radar dish. So the NSA put a bunch of giant radar dishes in orbit.

The Internet explosion of the nineties was like Halloween and Christmas combined for the NSA. For most of that decade, something like 99 percent of all Internet traffic was routed through the United States, making it a cinch to scoop up every bit of it as it floated by. By 1999, there must have been entire mental wards full of NSA analysts driven mad by terabytes of *Star Trek* fan fiction.

Today, ECHELON may be nearing the end of its life. In the last decade, the worldwide communications infrastructure has decentralized and returned to Earth, relying now on line-of-sight networks (you and I call them cellular networks) and fiber-optic cables. Neither technology relies on a central hub for routing traffic. To intercept all the cell phone traffic in the world, you'd need to place a listening device on every cell tower. To listen in on modern Internet traffic, you'd need to travel the globe physically tapping fiber-optic trunk cables.

Behemoth government programs like ECHELON don't ever die. The actual listening capability of ECHELON may be diminished, but the analytical kung fu it has learned is not something the NSA will lightly discard. It is certain that ECHELON will only transmogrify into some new technological terror designed to snoop into our secrets.

WHO INVENTED IT AND WHY?

It's pretty rare that individuals get credited with inventing giant, secret government programs. The budget and staff of the NSA are both classified, and for a long time the government refused to even admit there was such an agency. Their headquarters has its own exit off the freeway, leading directly to their enormous parking lot, which is guarded by very polite men with automatic weapons.

It's uncommon to hear the name of a former NSA employee. It's even more uncommon for those former employees to speak publicly about what they did for the NSA, since everything they do is classified and telling the *New York Times* about it could lead to charges of treason. There are a few names associated with ECHELON, but none so strongly as to be called its "inventor."

The "why" behind ECHELON is much more obvious. At the end of the World War II, everyone thought we were going to keep the party going by kicking Stalin's ass out of Europe and marching all the way to Moscow. All our stuff was in Europe already, and the army was eager to make a hat trick of Japan, Germany, and the Soviet Union.

Ultimately, the government decided that the world was better off if Eastern Europe wasn't turned into any more of a scorched wasteland than it already was, but everyone still figured war was just around the corner. Work began immediately on a system to listen to the Russians. That system, combined with other signals intelligence programs, eventually became ECHELON.

WHO'S USING IT TO WATCH YOU?

The government

Maybe not the government that rules the country you live in, but *a* government anyway. It's illegal for the NSA to spy on American citizens (not that that's ever really stopped them), just like it's illegal for British foreign intelligence agencies to spy on their citizens. It is not, technically, illegal for British intelligence to spy on American citizens and then tell the NSA what they heard, and vice versa.

Government agencies—especially spy agencies—love having "deniability." Deniability is great. It's when everyone knows you've done something bad, but no one can prove it.

When you capture an enemy soldier, you might move him around, passing him through the hands of various agencies from allied countries. You might end up leaving him alone for a few days in a secret Polish prison under the care of, let's say, Turkish secret police. If, when your captive is handed back over to you, he is missing some teeth or fingernails and accompanied by a dossier of information on enemy troop movements, who are you to say what happened? If he was tortured, it wasn't your fault! You weren't even there! Blame the Turks! Deniability.

The same thing goes for domestic spying. When you have an intelligence-sharing agreement and share an apparatus like ECHELON with other countries, it's entirely plausible that there may be a tacit agreement to spy on each others' citizens and hand over regular reports. There's no reason to say where the information came from, only that it may be relevant to everyone's security.

The NSA has displayed little shyness in recent years about illegally spying on American citizens. But before that, it probably just got its information on us from England.

WHY IS IT WATCHING YOU?

That's an interesting question. For fifty years, the government and just about everyone else was convinced that a cataclysmic war was imminent. ECHELON was created in the hope of understanding the Soviets well enough to head off such a war. If that proved impossible, we could learn enough about what they planned to attack first with overwhelming destructive force.

That world was easy for agencies like the NSA to understand because the bad guys more or less played by the same set of rules as we did. Since the collapse of the Soviet Union, though, the intelligence environment has become much more confusing. Terrorists gather together in secretive, decentralized organizations with few ties to a country. They don't use traditional means of military communication, and they hide among the civilian population.

To normal people, it's terrifying that anyone on the street could be planning to blow up a subway station. For intelligence agencies, it's just frustrating. They used to be able to pin the enemy down and put him under a microscope. Now it's all they can do to even find rumors about where the enemy might be. If the enemy could be anyone, the best solution is to watch everyone.

Of course, your safety is not our intelligence agencies' only motivating factor. In 2001, the European Parliament issued a report warning businesses in the European Community to begin encrypting their communications because they believed ECHELON had been used for industrial espionage. That's right: The NSA was shaking the dust off its signals analysis calculator to financially benefit American businesses. It has also been alleged that ECHELON was used to spy on Japanese automakers to give Detroit an edge.

Unless you're a millionaire European industrialist (or a billionaire American one), this doesn't mean much to you. Except, if the NSA is willing to engage in what is essentially an act of war against our closest allies only to benefit American corporations, what might they be willing to do to you?

WHY SHOULD YOU BE WORRIED ABOUT IT?

There's a mantra among proponents of secret domestic spying: "If you've done nothing wrong," they say, "you've got nothing to worry about." Even if the government is listening in on your telephone conversations, nothing bad will happen to you unless you're a terrorist or a drug dealer.

Of course, the logic of the statement runs counter to both the Fourth (protection from unreasonable search and seizure) and Fifth (due process, protection from self-incrimination) amendments. Such surveillance is a fundamental violation of our civil rights—rights that criminals and terrorists have, too.

The right to privacy is one of the foundations of a free and functioning democracy. Without the expectation of privacy in our personal communications, it becomes impossible for us to act freely. There's a reason totalitarian states keep a close eye on their citizens—if people know they're being watched, they won't misbehave. If the government is already collecting information on everyone, it's a short step from busting drug dealers to hassling political dissidents, religious dissenters, or social freaks. If they're checking up on everyone, how do they differentiate between agents of a terrorist organization actually planning an attack and teenage anarchists chatting idly about the overthrow of their school principal?

You should be *very* afraid of programs like ECHELON. Because when any part of the government begins ignoring the rights of its citizens, we have begun to lose our freedom.

WHAT CAN YOU DO ABOUT IT?

Not much, unfortunately

No one really knows the full capabilities of the ECHELON network. It has been in operation for a half century. ECHELON may be rapidly approaching obsolescence, unable to deal with newer fiber-optic and cellular technology.

However, it has evolved and adapted to new communications technology in the past, adding capabilities as needed to keep up with the pace of change. The only purpose of the NSA and its counterpart organizations in other countries is to develop the means to listen in on our enemies, no matter what means of communication they use. The diversity and rapid pace of change present in Europe and the United States make for an ideal testing ground for new methods of interception and analysis. Any new techniques or technologies developed will probably be deployed in the western world first, just to make sure they work.

If you want to maintain the high-tech lifestyle you are no doubt used to, there's very little you can do to avoid the all-seeing eye of ECHELON.

Call your senator

The United States Senate has a committee devoted to the oversight of the American intelligence community. It's true they're politicians, so we can't expect much, but one thing is true of all senators: They hate getting calls from the public. It's the worst part of the job, mostly because the majority of the calls they get are from crazy or paranoid people who have nothing better to do than complain. It's very rare that anyone calls to give them props for a job well done—which is aggravated by the fact that so few of them actually do their job well.

Senators love flexing their fiduciary muscles. The Senate Select Committee on Intelligence performs an annual review of the president's proposed intelligence budget. If given the proper motivation, they will threaten the budgets of individual agencies.

If you've got a senator on the SSCI, give him or her a call. Let your lawmaker know you don't like being spied on. Tell him that you're not willing to sacrifice your right to privacy just on the off chance that one of your neighbors is a terrorist. Even if neither of your senators is on the committee, chances are they have some friends on it. Call them both, explain your objections, and urge them to scold the NSA. Try to avoid profanity or sounding crazy during the call. Being reasonable and rational is a great way to get through to senators. It's a change from the calls they usually get.

Understand, however, that the NSA will probably ignore anything the Senate says to them. In fact, when the SSCI demands the agency's representatives come by and explain themselves, they often don't even show up. Like the rest of us, the NSA doesn't have much respect for the Senate.

Act like a terrorist

The irony of all this domestic spying is that it's done in the hope of catching terrorists, but terrorists know what to do to avoid being spied on. Systems like ECHELON tend only to catch really stupid terrorists.

Stay on the move. Don't live in one place for more than a few days. Never use your name or speak your location over unencrypted communications. Ditch the land line and rely exclusively on a mobile phone, preferably one a few years old with no Internet capabilities or, even better, prepaid burners from a drug store that you only use for one or two calls before throwing them away. Don't go online except from Internet cafes that let you pay in cash (use small bills to minimize your exposure to RFID-tagged money), and when you do, use an IP anonymizer. It's not a comfortable or fun way to live, but that's kind of the point, right?

CHAPTER 7

NAZI DOCTORS, SEX DISEASES, AND LSD— THE SECRET HISTORY OF EXPERIMENTS ON HUMAN BEINGS

The CIA promises it no longer kidnaps people in order to subject them to sexual torture and psychotropic drugs. So we can all breathe a sigh of relief. Because if you can't trust the CIA, who can you trust?

THREAT LEVEL

WHAT IS IT?

For nearly 100 years, the U.S. military and intelligence communities experimented on American citizens, soldiers, children, convicts, and the citizens of other countries. The populace of the United States has been attacked by chemical and biological agents deployed by the CIA, drugged by doctors on the payroll of the army, sprayed with toxic chemicals by the navy, and injected with radioactive materials by the Atomic Energy Commission.

It began in 1900 in the Philippines. Army doctors infected five prisoners with the black plague (which, you'll recall from high school history, killed pretty much everyone in the world in the 1300s), and induced a condition called beriberi in another twenty-nine. Beriberi causes chronic pain, insanity, heart failure, and death. Good times for everyone involved.

During World War I, more than a million casualties were caused by the deployment of chemical agents like mustard gas, phosgene gas, and chlorine gas—terrible weapons that can drown your lungs in blood, destroy your ability to breathe, or sear the flesh from your bones. The widespread use of chemical weapons during the war inspired military scientists to "test" protective gear by putting it on soldiers and making them sit in rooms filled with poison gas.

In the 1930s, the U.S. government fell in love with syphilis. It's easy to understand: Syphilis was the haute couture of neurodegenerative sex diseases. For hundreds of years, it had run rampant among all the top celebrities. Oscar Wilde, van Gogh, Tolstoy, Ivan the Terrible, Batman (okay, well, not *that* Batman—John Batman, an Australian pioneer), Napoleon, and Al Capone all had the pox. Even Hitler got in on the action, though he only did it because it was popular and he was a poseur.

The Public Health Service (part of what is now the U.S. Department of Health and Human Services) wanted to know how syphilis worked, so for forty years, starting in 1932, they tracked 400 African-American men with the disease. These men were the poorest of the poor, the sons and grandsons of slaves. Most of them were sharecroppers scraping by on miniscule plots for a crop that barely kept them fed and clothed. Many were illiterate, and all of them had become infected with the disease through ignorance.

The PHS, which had access to enough penicillin to treat every one of these men, allowed the disease to run its course. The men infected their wives, who infected their children. For four decades, these men and their families suffered from a disease that causes painful skin lesions, weakens the bones, rots the mind, and eventually kills. In exchange for their suffering, the men received free meals and medical care for anything other than syphilis.

Widening the net

Of course, the Tuskegee Syphilis Experiment is only the most famous bit of syphilitic fun the Public Health Service had. In the late forties, they took the act on the road, heading to Guatemala, where infected prostitutes were supplied to prison inmates, mental patients, and soldiers. Later on, researchers got bored waiting on traditional infection vectors, so they infected hundreds of people by just dumping the disease into open wounds.

The government agency responsible for the health and well-being of American citizens wasn't the only one doing this. Starting in the late forties, after the horrendous aftereffects of atomic attacks began to become apparent in Japan, the United States Atomic Energy Commission got in the game. Their first project, in a joint venture with the Quaker Oats company, involved feeding radioactive oatmeal to mentally handicapped children at a place called the Fernald School in Massachusetts—less a school than a prison for mentally disabled kids.

Throughout the fifties and sixties, the AEC continued to inject radioactive material into people to test their reactions. In several experiments across the country, they used severely injured or ill people, children, and pregnant women as test subjects for all sorts of toxic or radioactive material.

In 1950, the U.S. Navy opened up a whole new chapter in government experimentation on humans when it burst balloons over San Francisco that contained a biological agent called *Serratia marcescens*. This bacteria can cause urinary tract infections, pink eye, and potentially deadly infections of the heart valves. The subsequent decade saw attacks by the Atomic Energy Commission (radioactive chemicals sprayed over 2,000 square kilometers in Washington), the CIA (whooping cough released from boats near Tampa Bay), and the Army (attacks on cities in the United States and Canada ranging from aerial deployment of toxic chemical agents to the purposeful release of mosquitoes infected with yellow fever).

The big, bad boys

These are just bit players in a drama starring the original gangsta of human experimentation projects in the United States—that bad mamajama, the Sultan of CIA psychedelics, the King of Cruel and Unusual—MKULTRA. MKULTRA was the ultimate secret torture playground of the CIA, with a toolbox that looked like a combination between an Abu Ghraib photo studio and Hunter S. Thompson's car trunk.

You've probably heard of MKULTRA; it's the program that dosed a bunch of soldiers with LSD in the fifties, hoping to discover a new method of brainwashing or mind control. The picture most of us have is of a CIA so totally out of touch with reality that it fixates on psychotropic drugs as a means of creating psychic super spies. We assume they must have been testing too much of their own product; they'd been blinded by mushroom-fueled dreams of unkillable telekinetic *übermenschen*; the walls at CIA headquarters were covered in black light posters of Hendrix; and that sloppily written briefs about chakras and third eyes passed from hand to hand along with a glass pipe and a bag of chronic.

The reality is, the CIA was established in 1947 with a single mandate—to rock the USSR's face so hard it would melt completely off. This was the purpose and the prize. The CIA never once lost sight of it.

To the spook community, the Nazis had been a warm-up exercise. The Soviet Union was a true evil empire—a totalitarian monster superstate, determined to plunge the planet into an unending hell of repression, deprivation, and misery. Today, we remember the Soviet Union as a tottering framework—outmoded and outmaneuvered by the West, ready to collapse under its own weight at any moment, and only held together by the iron will of the psycho in charge. But back in the fifties, the USSR was an unbeatable world-conquering superpower. We stood against them when the rest of the world refused, risking life and limb to protect a planet that did not see the danger we did. The communists had stared us down in Europe, were fighting us to a standstill in Korea, and within the next couple of decades they would hold us off near Cuba and chase us out of Vietnam. The spread of communism was inevitable. To stop it, any price was worth paying.

To that end, the newly formed CIA became one of the prime beneficiaries of something called Project Paperclip. This program was intended to deny the expertise of German scientists to the Soviet Union by spiriting them away from the war tribunals at Nuremberg, erasing all evidence of crimes they'd committed, and putting them to work inventing nightmares for the United States.

The agency wasted no time. Starting in 1947, a whole litter of projects devoted to mind control, interrogation, and brainwashing was birthed. By 1953, the CIA was busily trying to discover a means of chemically brainwashing enemy agents. Thousands of citizens and soldiers were dosed unwittingly with drugs like mescaline, LSD, scopolamine, and morphine. People were beaten, starved, forcibly addicted to drugs, hypnotized, and deprived of sleep.

The programs were so numerous, ambitious, and wide ranging that managing all of them became difficult. MKULTRA was launched to give the CIA's mind control programs a management infrastructure. Bringing these various programs under a single umbrella made diverting black-budget funds and acquiring test subjects much easier. Under MKULTRA, the programs continued to expand.

Counterintelligence researchers studied methods of torture and coercion used by Chinese and Soviet agencies, seeking to devise ways to either defeat them or improve them. Experimental whorehouses in San Francisco and New York dosed nonconsenting subjects with drugs, photographed sexual liaisons for the purposes of blackmail, and more. Subproject 68 induced months-long comas in mental patients, locked others in sensory isolation for weeks or months at a time, and subjected still more to days or weeks strapped into a blacked-out football helmet listening to a single repeated message. People from all walks of life—soldiers and civilians, adults and children, men and women—were subjected to dangerous drugs, sexual abuse, and physical and psychological torture. Drugs and torture methodologies perfected on American citizens were deployed against enemy agents around the world. Techniques developed by MKULTRA, including sleep deprivation and sensory assault, are still in use today.

For twenty-two years, MKULTRA continued its work. In 1973, the program was ended and the vast majority of its records destroyed. We know of the program because of a Congressional investigation and because a handful of documents were missed by the destruction order issued by then-director Richard Helms.

The demise of MKULTRA did not mean the end of human experimentation by the United States government. In 2005, Homeland Security released a "nontoxic gas" into the New York subway system to track how a chemical attack might disperse. Meticulous records have been kept of interrogation practices used at Guantanamo Bay. Physicians monitored waterboarding, offering suggestions for protecting the health of the subjects and maximizing their discomfort.

There is no reason to believe that the CIA or any other government agency is any less willing to experiment on civilians than they once were. Exceptions written into part of Title 50 in the U.S. Code allow the Department of Defense to engage in biological and chemical experimentation on American civilians. The law insists that each subject must give informed consent to the testing—which means that everyone involved has to be dumb enough to sign up for anthrax testing for it to be legal. Congress frowns on voters getting gassed.

These days, it's corporations that do the testing, though generally on a much smaller scale. In 1998, Dow Chemical paid a bunch of college students $460 each to eat pills filled with the active ingredient in Raid. That's the price of a top-notch smartphone and a nice dinner, in exchange for eating nerve gas. Nummers!

Earlier this decade, Lockheed Martin asked volunteers to eat rocket fuel for six months. For half a year of consuming a chemical that can impede thyroid function and cause infant retardation, volunteers got paid a whopping $1,000. That's less than two months' worth of groceries for a family of four. But then, the rocket fuel was provided free of charge, and I hear it's quite filling.

Bizarre, unethical, potentially harmful tests on Americans continue, both in public and in secret. Feeling lightheaded? Suffering mood swings? Experiencing a sudden burning sensation? Hearing things? It might not be you. It might be something in the air.

HOW DOES IT WORK?

If recent history is any guide, the government just goes ahead and does stuff and hopes no one notices. The last decade is like a greatest-hits list of things the government wished had been kept secret—torture, secret prisons, falsified intelligence, bizarre PR decisions—but bad decision-making was not invented by the last two administrations. Sexual misconduct, arms sales to terrorists, use of chemical weapons in Vietnam, illegal attacks on Cambodia, burglary, assassination, CIA training of South American death squads—all of these things were done on the simple assumption that no one would notice.

MKULTRA and similar projects are no exception. The documentation associated with MKULTRA was all classified Top Secret, but most of the experimentation was done at universities, military bases, and hospitals—none of them secure facilities. In the case of most modern human experimentation, secrecy is driven by shame. Whether they feel guilt or not, the bureaucrats and scientists involved in human experimentation are unlikely to ever admit the role they played. The fallout would destroy their lives, burying them under lawsuits, annihilating their careers, and subjecting them to the revulsion of their peers.

They further enforced secrecy by the selection of an appropriate subject population. Convicts, soldiers, and mental patients are popular subjects because they are captive populations, bound by the orders of their superiors or caregivers. Little attention is paid by loved ones or relatives to the treatment of criminals or the insane, and soldiers are indoctrinated into a culture of loyalty and silence, especially in the face of pain and discomfort.

The extremely poor are another popular subject population. Lacking access to health care and education, they possess a winning combination of need and ignorance. They are often willing to sacrifice anything to provide basic necessities for their families. The poor are used to being sick; if they suddenly feel sicker, it is only an expansion of the discomfort they probably already feel, and at least now they have the nice men in the white coats to provide medical care.

People are lured into experimentation by the promise of money, the possible cure of an incurable disease, access to resources they otherwise wouldn't have, or even a desire to contribute to the common good. Once in an experimental framework, the subjects are kept isolated, either physically by locking them in a facility (another reason convicts and mental patients are such great subjects), or socially through blackmail, bribery, or other forms of coercion. Without access to the world outside the experiment, the subjects cannot seek assistance from noninvolved medical professionals, the media, or their families. They become dependent on the people running the experiment.

If a subject is given any explanation at all, it is a lie designed to cover the true nature of the experiment. If the subject survives, shame, guilt, or insanity combined with her ignorance as to the true nature of her experience will prevent her going public. Drastic, chronic mental and physical problems, including depression, suicide, birth defects, schizophrenia, a drastically shortened lifespan, and organ or brain damage can all afflict the subject, downgrading her threat as a security risk even further.

WHO INVENTED IT AND WHY?

The Nazis get a lot of credit for perfecting the modern evil experiment, and make no mistake, they did a lot to advance the cause of twentieth-century mad science. The Nazis excelled in cruelty, killing thousands in bizarre experiments in only a few years, and disfiguring thousands more. But they did not invent this kind of human experimentation. In fact, at the Nuremberg trials, some Nazi doctors cited early twentieth-century American work as an inspiration.

In the nineteenth century, it was not uncommon for medical researchers to test theories on slaves. For hundreds of years before that, criminals were popular test subjects, and the sick or diseased were often considered mobile laboratories for even the most bizarre theories. Scientific curiosity and sociopathy have often traveled hand in hand.

MKULTRA was managed by a club-footed doctor named Sidney Gottleib. Gottleib was a chemist with a weird passion for poisons, and a finger in some of the strangest pies ever baked by the CIA. He devised plans to chemically attack Fidel Castro's beard, occasionally spiked people's drinks with LSD (even when he wasn't experimenting on them), planted electrodes in people's brains, and may have been part of a CIA program to find psychics and fortune tellers to use as spies.

Gottleib's boss was CIA director Allen Dulles. He was a career bureaucrat and lawyer from a family of public servants. His brother, after whom one of Washington's airports is named, was Eisenhower's secretary of state. Dulles was a straight-laced government operative who'd climbed the ranks of the bureaucracy like many others before him, serving as a diplomat, intelligence coordinator, and field agent. It was his vision and resolve that justified twenty years of organized torture by the CIA.

After Dulles retired, two other men held the reins of the CIA before Richard Helms took over in 1966, but it was Helms who would be most closely associated with MKULTRA. Helms was a born spy—tight-lipped, morally flexible, unafraid to pay the high prices Cold War intelligence work demanded. During World War II, he served as a field agent with the Office of Strategic Services. After the war, he ran counterintelligence in several countries in Eastern and Central Europe, a job that must have been bloody as hell. He joined the CIA the year it was formed.

While serving as a CIA spook, and then its director, Helms enlisted mafia hit men and mutinous soldiers in assassination attempts against Fidel Castro and Chile's Salvador Allende; funded the destabilization of democratic governments; planned kidnappings; and supplied poison, money, and weapons to violent extremists around the globe. In 1973, with media scrutiny of the agency mounting and pressure from the president to use agency assets to cover up Nixon's links to Watergate (which Helms refused to do), he ordered MKULTRA shut down and all evidence of it destroyed. Thousands of documents were shredded, leaving only spotty records of its legacy.

WHO'S USING IT TO WATCH YOU?

The government. Again!

The government is intensely interested in your health; specifically, how healthy you are and how easy it is to affect that. They want to know all they can about what kills you or makes you sick or drives you crazy, and how those things move through the population or flow through the nation's infrastructure.

This is crucial knowledge. It is a matter of preparation—for attacks, for pandemics, or for simple civil unrest. The government—and especially the military—must be on the bleeding edge of science to ensure an advantage against all enemies, present and future. The justification for assault on American citizens has always been that sacrifices must be made in the name of security. This is an excuse you must be used to hearing by now, that your individual rights are secondary to the good of the body politic, that you must sacrifice your privacy, your freedom, and even your health, so that the government can ensure your safety.

Corporations, especially the huge, sort-of-evil ones

Corporations are constantly complaining about government regulation, and with good reason. Regulation forces them to behave in a manner that is not always conducive to growing the bottom line. Government agencies like the FDA and the EPA insist that companies make industrial and consumer products that are mostly nontoxic and don't murder everyone, a requirement that makes the manufacture of things like nerve gas and explosives costly and difficult.

One of the ways in which corporations can head off government regulations is to conduct human trials proving, more or less, that poisonous things aren't that poisonous. The EPA and the FDA receive studies every year from chemical companies, weapons manufacturers, the oil and tobacco industries, and others, all showing that their products aren't really hideously deadly and that it's the dead person's fault he got so exposed to dioxins or radiation or toxic smoke.

Industry watches us very closely, hoping to arrive at alternative conclusions to those reached by real scientists. When you make billions of dollars a year pooping toxic smoke into the air, spending a few thousand dollars conning volunteers into eating poison is a pretty tiny slice off the bottom line.

Scientists

Scientists are mostly good guys. Without scientists, we wouldn't have things like computers, 3-D movies, aspirin, and fart-free cucumbers. But scientific curiosity can sometimes get out of hand. When you're deep into the discovery of the answer to an ages-old question, it can be easy to lose sight of what is reasonable.

A successful scientist is a hyper-focused, detail-oriented savant. He is able to ignore all irrelevant detail in favor of data that strengthens or weakens a hypothesis. When his material, whether it is men, machines, or minerals, protests, he must be able to divorce himself, at least a little bit, from his humanity. He must focus on the evidence.

Modern medical trials are an excellent example. They operate under strict ethical guidelines and require informed consent from all participants, but they also demand a control group—a selection of subjects who will receive a placebo in the place of the treatment being tested. The researchers conducting the trial can be absolutely convinced of a drug's efficacy, but to be scientifically certain, some people must be allowed to continue suffering (at least until a certain point—compassionate use protocols dictate that if a drug appears to be working as expected the control group is administered proper treatment). This is critical for the advancement of medical science, a vital sacrifice for the greater good. To the scientist, the answer to the question being asked must be paramount. For researchers isolated by secrecy, it must be easy to lose touch with the humanity of their subjects.

This is apparent in the lab reports and transcripts that survive from MKULTRA, as well as the testimony of Nazi scientists at the Nuremberg tribunals. It's difficult as a normal person to understand, but most of these men were not pure evil; nor were they simply following orders. They were only men—men who lost sight of the rational horizon. They became divorced from the fundamental humanity of their subjects, using dehumanizing terms like "the material" (MKULTRA), serial numbers (Nazis), or plain initials (MKULTRA again). They became obsessed with the answer to a question and lost track of everything else.

WHY IS IT WATCHING YOU?

Human experimentation is almost always done in the name of the people. MKULTRA worked to develop interrogation, brainwashing, and counterintelligence techniques. Americans were attacked and tortured, ostensibly to make America safe from Communist infiltration. For half a century, we lived under a constant existential threat; long enough that these days, if we don't feel like someone is planning to kill us, we start to get really uncomfortable.

The government, we are told, needs to experiment on people to keep them safe. They need to know exactly how the communists/terrorists/South American drug gangs will come after us so that they can defend us. They say that the only way they can protect us from torture, brainwashing, and biological attack is to be better at it than the bad guys.

The motivations of corporations are less pure but also less perverse. There was a time when companies felt a patriotic duty to team up with the government and help fund tests like the radioactive oatmeal project, but that time is long past. These days, everything contributes to the bottom line. When millions or billions of dollars are at stake, the health and safety of individuals quickly becomes immaterial. If feeding rat poison to children will potentially open up a new profit center, those kids quickly become commodities.

Modern human trials are run primarily by pharmaceutical companies. The prescription drug industry is worth hundreds of billions of dollars. Being the first to bring a new drug to market can mean billions more. In a room packed with that much money, there is no space for concern about the well-being of other people.

Fortunately, pharmaceutical companies operate under extremely strict testing guidelines, but the same cannot be said of tests run on substances without medical applications. When Dow wants to test a chemical on human beings, no government funding of the test means no government oversight. If the results are never submitted to the government, the test and its consequences could remain secret forever.

WHY SHOULD YOU BE WORRIED ABOUT IT?

For 100 years, the government and corporations have been testing poisons, drugs, diseases, weapons, and torture methods on people. They have dosed us with everything from LSD to nerve gas. They have infected us with syphilis, addicted us to heroin, fed us bug spray, and beaten us into unconsciousness. Most of this they have done in secret, without our consent.

The history of unethical human experimentation stretches back centuries, and includes countries around the world. For hundreds of years, people have been injected with diseases, covered in leeches, bled, amputated, and exorcised.

Things like this are rarely done anymore, but why? Is it because governments and corporations realized what they were doing was wrong? Did the factors that motivated these tests disappear? Or is it because they started to worry they'd be caught? MKULTRA ended because media scrutiny of the CIA meant discovery was inevitable.

Today, just as in the Cold War, the government is afraid. Terrorists hide in every shadow. Corporations with global reach have discovered that financial clout brings with it a measure of invulnerability from consequence. Competition for every dollar is more fierce now than ever before.

Confronted with the threat of terrorists, what shenanigans might the government get up to in secret? Given the possibility of making an extra $100 billion, what might a corporation be willing to do?

WHAT CAN YOU DO ABOUT IT?

Don't volunteer

Modern experiments, even the strange, unethical ones, require willing volunteers. Research trials can be an excellent source of income should you meet the subject criteria, but they can also mean dire physical or mental side effects. The advance of medicine requires human volunteers, but nothing about science requires the ignorance of its subjects. When and if you are given a consent form, read it carefully (or have your lawyer do so), and never be afraid to ask questions. If you don't like the answers you get, get the hell out of there.

Watch the skies

Should the CIA or the military decide to spray your home town with toxic gas, they will need to do so from boats or airplanes, or via remote devices planted to maximize dispersal. As the saying goes, if you see something, say something. The suspicious packages or individuals you're supposed to be looking for might not be terrorists; they might just be Homeland Security agents running a biowarfare attack on your favorite local deli.

CHAPTER 8

SKIN, SALIVA, AND FOOTPRINTS— HOW YOUR BODY BETRAYS YOU

Everywhere you go, you leave a gross little trail of skin flakes, hair, and fibers from your clothing. Your body is a walking pile of slowly degrading garbage that the government can easily use to follow you.

THREAT LEVEL

WHAT IS IT?

For years, TV detectives have been gathering the skin, blood, and semen of TV criminals. The evidence always tells a story full of twists and turns, but it always leads to the right guy. On television, genetics never lie, fingerprints are easily identified, and the real bad guy is always convicted on the strength of the evidence he leaves behind.

In real life, forensics is not terribly sexy. Mostly, it means taking photos or plaster casts of footprints (by far the most plentiful trace evidence at any crime scene). Even the fun blood-pathology stuff is done by putting a tiny bit of evidence in a test tube and then waiting while a computer does something. It is, like most science, boring. (Unless you're a scientist, in which case it's terribly exciting.)

It can, however, tell an investigator a surprising amount. Our understanding of genetics has progressed to the point that we can trace the origins of entire racial groups to individuals who lived thousands of years ago. For a few hundred dollars, you can have your entire genome mapped in a couple of hours. The markers for specific diseases (Parkinson's), physical expressions (redhead), and predilections (alcoholism) can all be recognized and flagged. Your blood, your hair, and your saliva all carry your genetic history. The question is, now that we have access to this information, what do we do with it? Will insurance companies demand a gene sequence before agreeing to insure you? Will they charge extra to insure you for diseases from which your genes say you might someday suffer?

Your genes aren't the only part of you a properly equipped researcher can mine for information. Biometrics like fingerprints and eyes and the pattern of a voice are relied on as forms of identification. Tiny shreds of clothing and the tread patterns of your shoes can be analyzed, and their origins and owner determined. If you are a criminal, everything you own, from toothbrushes to tube socks, becomes potential evidence. But investigators can also be fooled. DNA evidence can be easily planted, fingerprints can be faked or misidentified, voices can be mimicked. All that you are can be turned against you.

HOW DOES IT WORK?

In a forensic investigation, the investigator is trying to build a profile of you. The first piece of evidence he will look for is your footprint. You scatter these behind you in abundance. Every time you walk into a room with mud or dust on the bottom of your shoe, every time you cross your lawn, and every time you step in the blood of your victims, you leave a footprint behind you. An analyst can discover a wealth of information about you in the swoops and curves of your shoe bottom.

Computerized databases instantly match the make and model of a shoe. Your weight, height, and the way you walk become public knowledge. The spacing and smudging of footprints indicate your mental state—are they erratic and repetitive, indicating panic? Or are they the measured steps of perfect calm? Their placement helps create a narrative of the sequence of events. Dirt shed from the bottom of your shoe is used to determine where you came from. If it occurs to you to ditch your footwear, don't. Even more information can be gleaned by looking at the impression your foot makes inside your shoe. Thinking of trying to hide the evidence of your passage by sticking strictly to carpet? Don't bother. Electrostatic dust and ultraviolet light lift your footprints from a carpet the same way they lift fingerprints from glass.

Speaking of fingerprints, that's the next thing someone trying to profile you will look for. Your fingertips produce an oil you leave behind on every object you touch. Usually, the fingerprint becomes smudged as your fingers drag slightly across a surface, but sometimes a clear picture of one or more fingers is left behind. If you've got a touchscreen phone, look at it right now. See the streaks on it? Finger grease. That stuff gets everywhere.

It's true that no two fingerprints are the same, but that includes prints taken from the same finger on the same hand only moments apart. Skin is flexible, which means your fingertip distorts slightly every time you press it to a surface. The identification of a fingerprint is more art than science, reliant on the guesswork of skilled individuals and expert computer systems, and with a false positive rate as high as 20 percent, giving you a solid one-in-five chance of being fingered as a serial killer.

Fingerprints captured in the wild are called latent prints. When an object is found that is likely to have a usable print on it, the surface is covered with either a fine dust or chemical agent that reacts with the sweat in the prints. This increases the contrast between the surface and the print, rendering the print visible. It can then be photographed or lifted on a thin plastic film for later analysis.

Little pieces of you

At a crime scene, the most common DNA evidence comes in the form of bodily fluids like blood or semen, or from hair. The average person sheds about one and a half pounds of skin a year, microscopic flakes that disappear into the carpet. Unless the criminal in question has eczema, differentiating victim from perp from passerby using only skin flakes could be the work of a lifetime. The best bet for acquiring a suspect's DNA is by pulling hair or other material from the scene, skin or sweat in discarded clothing, blood from wounds inflicted by a victim, or other bodily fluid evidence. Finding any of this can be difficult, painstaking work, and it only sometimes pays a dividend.

Your house is a different story. Someone trying to build a genetic profile of you could snatch all they needed from your garbage can. It's certain that your saliva or hair is in your kitchen and bathroom garbage, and even badly degraded samples can be reconstructed into genetic profiles. Indoors, your toothbrush, your comb, your razor, and all those pounds of skin you've dumped on the floor over the years are available.

When the police build a DNA profile, they do not sequence the entire genome. Instead, they use a system called Short Tandem Repeat Analysis. This method recognizes that most of the human genome is basically identical from person to person. The variation from person to person is only about half a percent, which means you only need to look at a very tiny bit of DNA to find what is unique about it. It also means that very little detail about a person is revealed. DNA profiles do not include eye color, predispositions for diseases, or even ethnicity. They can be used to find familial relationships by comparison with other profiles, but other than that they contain about as much information as a fingerprint, just with a much higher degree of accuracy.

Having established the uniqueness of a sample, the investigator then needs to match that sample with a suspect. If they already think they know who committed a crime, that person can be compelled by a search warrant to submit to a cheek swab. If the DNA matches, they have someone to accuse.

If someone is attempting to profile you for reasons other than a criminal investigation, they may want to sequence your entire genome. For about $400, they can. Within a very short time, your profiler will have a complete genetic map of you—total access to your ancestry, potential health issues you might have, drug resistances, allergies, and more. All of that information comes from only a small fraction of the three billion base pairs in human DNA. As our understanding of genetic markers deepens, more and more information about you will become available, and much of that information will not be the sort of thing you want in the hands of strangers.

The ease of sequencing

Gathering this information is, from a computational perspective, simply a matter of brute force. The reason the Human Genome Project took ten years to complete a sequencing that can be done in a few hours today was because the computational resources that could be brought to bear when it began were a tiny fraction as formidable as those currently available. What it took a supercomputer to do ten years ago your microwave can do today. Now that computers know what they're looking for in a human DNA strand, it's more or less a simple matter of counting to six billion. A single dedicated machine of sufficient power can sequence your DNA in less than a month; a network of similar machines can do it in only a few days or even hours.

Biometric identification systems rely on sophisticated pattern-recognition software to correctly identify specific traits and match them against a stored database. Whether it's a voice pattern, a fingerprint, retinal scan, or facial recognition system, it is simply looking for specific points of comparison between the sample and the set of authorized faces or fingers it has stored in its system. These are not complicated systems, but they also suffer from serious flaws.

WHO INVENTED IT AND WHY?

Examination of footprints is the oldest type of forensic analysis. Early man tracked both his prey and his enemies by their prints, determining numbers, health, and direction of travel by examination of the scuffed dirt and trampled grass left behind. Armies have always marched in a manner specifically designed to cover their numbers by using the footsteps of the men in back to obscure those of the men before. The modern science of forensic footprint analysis is an extension of ancient hunting skills.

In ancient Babylon and China, contracts were sealed with fingerprints, and the prints of criminals were taken and stored. By the year 300, the Chinese were using fingerprints as evidence in criminal trials, gathering hand and footprints from crime scenes and using them to convict suspects.

It was in 1880 that Dr. Henry Faulds, a Scottish physician working in Tokyo, first developed a method of recording fingerprints using ink, as well as inventing a method to match latent prints to purposely recorded ones. An Englishman, Sir Francis Galton, devised the method of fingerprint classification that is used today, and an Argentinian police officer named Juan Vucetich created the first database of prints (on paper, in 1892). Finally, in 1902, a French cop named Alphonse Bertillon (who also invented the mugshot), devised a means of lifting a print off a surface, and modern fingerprint analysis was born.

It was only natural that fingerprint authentication for the purposes of security would arise from the practice of fingerprint analysis. Computerized fingerprint scanners have been available for decades.

Other forms of biometric identification systems weren't far behind. The idea that a retina could be used to identify a person was suggested in 1935 by a criminologist named Carleton Simon, but the technology wouldn't catch up to his ideas until the nineties. Work began on facial recognition in the late sixties, when a team of computer scientists and mathematicians were given a book of mugshots and asked to invent a machine that could match faces from two different pictures. It wasn't until 1997, however, that a workable means of fast, accurate face recognition was created.

DNA profiling and gene sequencing, like most modern scientific techniques, lack a single inventor. The techniques that gave rise to the current STR method of DNA profiling were first reported in 1984 in a paper written by a trio of researchers at the University of Leicester. Since then, hundreds of researchers and dozens of companies and universities have contributed to the continuing development of profiling techniques.

The first person to fully sequence a gene was a Belgian researcher named Walter Fiers, but that was just bacterial RNA—strictly the minor leagues. In fact, until fairly recently, sequencing the entire genome of a complex creature like a tube worm or a vole was so computationally intensive as to be functionally impossible. Until the nineties, computers simply didn't have the chops to deal with the amount of information encoded in a single strand of DNA.

The Human Genome Project, launched in 1990, involved dozens of research centers and hundreds of scientists working nonstop for a decade and cost $3 billion. Nowadays, some high-end toilets come with a combination bidet/gene sequencer, but in the year 2000, when the genome was finally published, it was a big deal.

The purpose of doing this was to answer fundamental questions about both the structure of DNA and how it expresses itself. Because of gene sequencing, we now know for certain that things like cancer, schizophrenia, and heart disease have a genetic component, what genes to look out for, and one day soon, how to fix them.

WHO'S USING IT TO WATCH YOU?

The 5-0

If you're a criminal, especially a violent one, the cops are tracking you right now, using every means at their disposal. They're cross-referencing any fingerprints they found at the scene of whatever crime you committed with local and national databases. If they picked up unique dirt from the bottoms of your shoes or fibers from your clothes, they're looking especially hard at fingerprint records for the locales indicated by that trace evidence. If your crime was heinous enough, or they believe you may be a foreign national, they are working with police departments in other countries to match your fingerprints.

Analysts identified the make, model, and size of your shoe right away. They know roughly how tall you are, how much you weigh, and whether you walk with a limp, pronate when you run, or if you have flat feet or high arches.

They've also built a DNA profile of you using hair or fluid found at the scene. They are searching the nearly seven million records contained in the United States government's Combined DNA Index System. If you've left genetic evidence at a previous crime scene (you incorrigible scamp!), you're probably listed there—if not by name, then at least by profile. If they have the DNA of any of your family members, then they know who those people are, too.

Even if you're not a criminal, there's a chance that the police have your fingerprints somewhere. Many local police departments hold fingerprinting drives at primary and high schools. The database of child-size prints these drives gather can be critical in solving kidnappings; but they're also quite useful in case one of those cute little kids grows up to be a complete bastard with the law on his tail.

The government

Depending on what countries you've lived in, the government may have your DNA on file. In the UK, the police and the government have extremely broad, poorly defined powers to collect DNA samples. The UK, with a population only about one-fifth the size of the United States, maintains a DNA database just as big as the one in the United States.

In the United States, police don't need a warrant to collect your DNA from a public place, like a used coffee cup at a cafe or a half-eaten hot dog at a ballpark. Logging every empty beer can on a frat house lawn for later DNA profiling is highly impractical, so the FBI and several states' police forces have begun taking DNA profiles in every arrest they make. If you've been booked, whether you were charged or not, the government might have your DNA.

Insurance companies

It isn't required yet, but it's easy to imagine a future in which insurance companies ask for a full gene sequence before they agree to insure you. Smokers often pay more for insurance; why not the same for those with a genetic predisposition to cancer? If you carry the markers for neurodegenerative disorders like Parkinson's or multiple sclerosis—diseases that can mean decades of expensive care and specialized prescriptions—your insurance company might write a specific exception into your policy. Just like homeowners in flood-prone areas pay extra for flood insurance, you'd end up ponying a premium to protect your error-prone brain.

Your boss

Many employers require drug tests. They're intended to weed out addicts, people so hooked on their substance of choice that they can't lay off for a couple days before filling the little cup. Those people tend to be unreliable, and in some workplaces can be dangerous. As gene sequencing becomes cheaper and cheaper, we can imagine a day in the very near future when a prospective employer requires applicants to submit their sequence. There, the markers for addiction, alcoholism, insanity, and chronic diseases that might affect performance could be noted and attached to your file. Someday very soon you might lose your job (or never get one) not because you're a drug addict, but because you could be.

WHY IS IT WATCHING YOU?

Fingerprint- and DNA-profile databases contain very little personalizing information, and therefore present little actual threat to your privacy. If you are ever the perpetrator or the victim of a crime, they could be used to identify you, but the potential for abuse is fairly low. Likewise, footprint evidence is generally only taken from a crime scene. Law enforcement agencies keep databases for the purpose of identifying footwear, but there is no permanent database recording individual footprints. Even if there were, it could only be used for the same purposes as a database of DNA profiles or fingerprints. For once, The Man is being honest when he says he's using the information he gathers to keep you safe.

At the moment, no one is really using full gene sequencing to watch you. It is the province of genealogy hobbyists and people interested in their likelihood of getting certain diseases. When you pay a company to sequence your genome, that information is turned over to you and the samples you provided are destroyed. If a company does retain your sequence, it does so anonymously.

WHY SHOULD YOU BE WORRIED ABOUT IT?

Footprint and fingerprint analysis are highly subjective. Both rely on human experts to reach conclusions. Humans, even experts, are notoriously fallible. There are scores of examples of people who were wrongly convicted based on corrupted or mistaken fingerprint evidence. Fingerprints and footprints smudge, smear, and degrade quickly in weather. Crime scenes can be easily contaminated by careless police or ignorant bystanders.

You've heard the claim that every person's fingerprints are unique, but no large-scale cross-referencing of fingerprints has ever been done. So when people claim every fingerprint is unique, they're only saying that because no one has ever found two identical fingerprints. Of the sixty-five billion fingerprints in the world, how many have been compared? There could easily be millions of identical or nearly identical fingerprints, and no one would ever know. You could, quite conceivably, have the same fingerprints as Osama bin Laden.

Likewise, common shoe brands can render footprint evidence less than useful. Nike sells millions of pairs of Air Force 1s every year. In some urban crime scenes, it's entirely feasible that similar or identical footprints made by perpetrators, victims, and totally uninvolved people could overlap. Imagine a crime scene at a sorority house—which pair of Ugg boots are you looking for?

On the flip side, some biometric identification technology can be easily defeated. Cheap fingerprint scanners can be defeated with super glue and a sheet of plastic foil. More expensive scanners can be hacked with false fingers made out of putty. Voice print identification systems can be spoofed with a high-fidelity recording. Face-recognition systems fall victim to high-resolution photographs. Retinal scanners are more secure than most systems, but they, too, can be defeated.

Biometric security is sexy because it's new and appears high-tech, but in the long term, it is less secure than a good password. When a password system is defeated, all you need to do is change the password. When a fingerprint identification system is defeated, well, you only get nine more resets before you have to go through the uncomfortable and costly procedure of having your hands replaced.

As previously mentioned, there are few laws protecting your DNA from collection; you leave it lying around everywhere. An agency or individual committed to building a broad, specific database could easily do so simply by picking up coffee cups at a local Starbucks. The trace DNA left on a coffee cup isn't going to be enough to sequence your genome, but it's more than enough to build a DNA profile.

Proper storage of even trace samples could leave the possibility of generating a full sequence at a later date open. As techniques and computing power continue to improve, partial or full sequences could be generated even from damaged samples. And suddenly, the FBI could know much more about you—eye color, hair color, health, and ethnicity.

If insurance companies or employers begin demanding gene sequences, the potential for abuse is vast. Choosing whether to insure or hire individuals based on genetic predispositions smacks of racism and eugenics, but it is also a very real possibility. Within the next few years, we just might be able to point to genetic markers for unemployment and bankruptcy—they'll be right next to the markers for alcoholism and cancer.

WHAT CAN YOU DO ABOUT IT?

Get crazy

The Unabomber wore shoes with soles from a smaller pair glued to the bottom. He was a complete loon, but he was also quite clever. Put the bottoms of a giant pair of Dunkmans on the bottom of your shoes and the cops will think they're chasing Shaq.

Wear gloves

This one's kind of a no-brainer, right? If you want to do something you shouldn't be doing and you want to make it harder for the law or whoever to catch you, don't leave your greasy handprints all over everything. Get a nice pair of rubber or leather gloves that are unlikely to rip or shed fiber traces, and go about your nefarious business.

Also, avoid being fingerprinted in the first place. If you're really that concerned about the government being able to identify you, don't give them the most obvious tool. If your fingerprints are already in a database somewhere, you might want to consider leaving the gloves on all the time.

Don't just throw away—incinerate!

Almost everything you throw away contains valuable trace evidence. What's more, once your trash is out on the sidewalk for the garbage collectors, it is no longer protected from unlawful search and seizure. So don't throw anything away—get yourself an incinerator and burn it all.

It's important to note that just building a bonfire in your yard or cooking everything in the barbecue grill may not be enough. Open fires do not burn hot enough to totally destroy all evidence of your existence. For true carbonization of your biometric record, you need the heat of an enclosed incinerator or wood stove. Once a batch of garbage burns down, stir the ashes and burn it again.

This goes double for your gloves and shoes. Whatever mischief you're getting up to, your gloves and shoes will bring home substantial evidence of it. Keep extra pairs. Destroy your current pair as often as you can afford.

Cut it off or cover it

You'll want to keep your hair short and well groomed to avoid shedding it everywhere. If you're trying to avoid being identified, the last thing you need is a wad of your luxurious mop static clinging to the ceiling over the scene of your latest caper. If you can't stand to cut off your beautiful locks, then keep them covered. Police and forensics professionals wear protective clothing that reduces the chance they will contaminate a crime scene with their own hair or skin. Depending on the budget of the force and the sensitivity of the crime scene, this protective clothing can range from face masks and rubber gloves to Tyvek environmental suits. You'll look like a headcase walking around in a paint suit, but it will keep most of your DNA in one place. And such suits burn fairly easily.

Blame someone else

The frame-up is the classic misdirection used when trying to avoid detection. The simplest explanation will always be the first course pursued by any agency investigating whatever mystery it is you leave in your wake. If you can leave a reasonably convincing false trail behind you, it could be enough to throw your pursuers off the scent.

Even if you get away from the authorities, you're certain to leave behind fingerprints and DNA traces. Luckily, if you're the sort of person who flees this kind of intense pursuit, you probably have a friend you don't mind betraying. This technique works especially well if your soon-to-be-ex-friend has a criminal record, a history of mental illness, or just a reputation for odd behavior. Gain access to his belongings. Replace your toothbrush, hairbrush or comb, razor, and favorite coffee mug with those belonging to your pal. These objects and ones like them—objects that are often handled and always have DNA samples on them—will be the first place the authorities check for your biometric traces. If they find several common objects that corroborate one another, they may be thrown off your trail and onto that of the guy I hope you're at least nice enough to visit in prison.

CHAPTER 9

THE REAL
TERMINATORS—
KILLER DRONES AND
MILITARY ROBOTS

They don't sleep. They don't eat. They've been armed and trained to kill. They're getting smarter all the time, and eventually one of them may come for you.

THREAT LEVEL

WHAT IS IT?

War zones crawl with semiautonomous killing machines armed with missiles, machine guns, and powerful metal claws. They are used for reconnaissance, bomb disposal, search and rescue, air-to-ground assault, and cargo transport. Half a dozen models are in service now, and half a dozen more are currently in development. The next wave of warfare will be done by remote control, and the wave after that will be fought by machines while we sit at home and watch on television.

The robots currently in the field range in size from the friendly, man-portable Packbot, weighing in at just over twenty-four pounds and just under three feet long to the enormous forty-four-foot, seven-ton Global Hawk reconnaissance drone. On the ground, the unarmed Packbot is just the smallest of a growing family of remote-operated tracked vehicles that will eventually range in size from a rich girl's purse dog up to the scale of a tank. Aerial drones already in service include the toy-sized FQM-151 Pointer and the Predator—famous as the preferred method for delivering Hellfire missiles through the windows of Pakistani mountain huts.

The TALON (a tracked robot similar to PackBot) can be configured to carry machine guns and grenade launchers, though it has yet to terrify live opponents with steely doom. PackBot and

TALON are primarily used to search for and dispose of bombs or for reconnaissance. High-quality video cameras that can see in infrared and pitch darkness and deft robot claws make them ideal for dealing with an IED without putting a soldier in harm's way. Both robots can climb stairs, crawl through sand and snow, live underwater, and operate up to a kilometer away from their controller. The top speed of these robots is around six miles an hour—slower than a running man, but your sprinter's pace doesn't matter when the robot has a rack of rifle grenades.

The Predator has been in service since 1995, first as a recon tool and more recently as an air-to-ground assault vehicle. It is whisper quiet and has a maximum altitude of about five miles. Using military satellites as relay stations, a Predator drone can be controlled by a pilot anywhere in the world. It can see through clouds, smoke, and sandstorms from its perch in the sky. It can be programmed to fly on its own, following a preplanned route and circling in a holding pattern once it arrives, where it can stay for nearly a full day before needing to land and refuel. Up to fourteen Hellfire missiles—each one capable of melting through tank armor—can be racked under the wings for delivery to an unsuspecting target's tea party. It is a smart, quiet, highly dangerous little aircraft with scores of kills to its name.

The defining characteristic of all of these robots is that they have a human at the wheel, and more importantly, holding the trigger. When it comes time for a robot to score a kill, a human being is the one making the decision. But that may change in the very near future. The Defense Advanced Research Projects Agency (DARPA—the agency that pays geniuses millions of dollars for coming up with insane new ways to wreck people's faces) has several projects in the works to put little robot brains in everything from bullets to helicopters. Current DARPA solicitations and projects include:

- Funding for sniper bullets that can find their own way into the brains of insurgents
- A semiautonomous HUMVEE that turns into a helicopter
- An unmanned variable airborne weapons platform (read: a small robot helicopter armed to its gnashing metal teeth) that follows soldiers around and dumps white phosphorus or missiles on the heads of anyone who shoots at them
- Expert systems that can analyze visual intelligence (like satellite videos and photos from recon drones) better than humans
- Rubber robots flexible enough to squeeze through keyholes and angry enough to strangle a dude
- Probably the most terrifying warfighting innovation since the smallpox-infected blanket—a robot that eats what it kills for fuel

Projects being developed independently of DARPA include little robot helicopters armed with shotguns, robotic snakes, and more.

DARPA also sponsors the DARPA Grand Challenge. Teams from all over the world send driverless vehicles out into punishing off-road or simulated urban courses. DARPA wants an expert system that can manage the chaotic and difficult task of driving from point A to point B—something most humans can barely manage to do—without asking for directions.

The goal is obvious: robots that can understand, interpret, and navigate terrain as easily and intelligently as the soldiers alongside whom they fight (or whom they replace). Someday soon, marines may not ever have to risk their lives clearing an insurgent hideout. Instead, a few small flying vehicles will zip in like a swarm of well-armed bees, scream through darkened halls shotgunning doors and clearing rooms with fragmentation grenades, and emerge into the sunlight to issue an after-action report to the commander lounging in the deck chair on the insurgent's lawn.

I wonder if the people who build combat robots lived through the entire 1980s without seeing a single movie.

HOW DOES IT WORK?

The control stations for most of the currently deployed drone vehicles are set up very similar to video game consoles, with a central display or displays connected to a dedicated hardware unit that runs the proprietary software brain of the drone. The controls are either a single joystick or the more familiar dual joystick setup of the Playstation or Xbox controller.

In the case of ground-based drones, the control signal is carried by radio, which relies on line of sight and relatively close proximity. The Predator and the Global Hawk (an unarmed recon drone) are typically controlled through secure microwave transmissions from military satellites. This greatly extends the range of control and reduces the chances of interception or interference by the enemy. When the pilot of a drone wants to fire a weapon, he must go through the same chain of command as any other pilot or soldier—he notifies command that a target has been sighted, declares if there are collateral targets or civilians around, and awaits permission.

As their systems improve and the military's understanding of robotic systems increases, drones will be given greater autonomy. Facial-recognition technology could allow robots to search for individual human targets. Bomb discovery and disposal could be fully automated. Larger robots built to haul heavy equipment could be taught to follow the soldiers to whom they are assigned, like an armored dog. Sophisticated friend or foe recognition capabilities could allow robots to make the distinction between ally and enemy and designate targets for human soldiers or human-operated drones. Inevitably, the decision to fire a killing shot will one day be fully automated.

WHO INVENTED IT AND WHY?

The first unmanned vehicle was designed and built in 1916 by an English inventor named Archibald Low. The English wanted an unmanned airplane they could load with explosives and crash into the Germans. You wouldn't call it a robot; more like a guided missile.

During World War II, several models of remote-operated aircraft came into use, mostly as practice targets for antiaircraft gunners. The first pilotless reconnaissance craft was probably a weather balloon with a camera dangling from it. What we think of today as Unmanned Aerial Vehicles weren't used in combat operations until the Vietnam War.

During the eighties, the CIA developed a sudden fever for small, quiet, unmanned spy planes. They wanted an unmanned vehicle that could replace the aging U2 spy plane—something that could quietly linger high in the sky and watch without being seen. At the time, there were several models of UAV to choose from, and all of them were outfitted with the latest in spy-camera technology. But they also all suffered from a relatively short range, a low maximum altitude, and engines that sounded like a South African soccer game. It wasn't until the early nineties that the CIA finally got what it wanted in the form of the General Atomics Predator.

With the use of the Predator in several war zones throughout the nineties, the utility of remote-operated vehicles and robots was proven. Nowadays, the military robot field is crowded with players like iRobot (PackBot), Foster-Miller (TALON), and a dozen other companies, all competing to make the tiniest, deadliest machine they can.

WHO'S USING IT TO WATCH YOU?

The government and all of its friends

In most cases, only governments can afford UAVs and combat robots. A Predator costs about $4.5 million before you add all the missiles at a cost of about $68,000 apiece. The PackBot runs somewhere around $60,000—very reasonable if you're in the market for a tough, partially amphibious search-and-rescue or bomb-disposal robot.

It isn't just the military and CIA that use drone aircraft. The United States's border with Mexico is patrolled constantly by Predator drones operated by Customs. The DEA doesn't have any Predators in service, but they may utilize smaller drone aircraft to patrol areas of the West Coast for drug fields.

As the Predator fleet ages and newer versions are phased into military service, it's likely drones will begin to enter the civilian sphere, first in service to law enforcement agencies and then to private concerns with an interest in maintaining an enduring presence in the sky. Cops, mapmakers, and even local news affiliates could end up operating Predators within the next decade.

Probably not corporations, for once

The primary civilian application for these kinds of robots is search and rescue. Infrared and night-vision cameras, high-end optics, and remote control allow rescue operations to run around the clock, in environments too treacherous for human crews. Robots like the TALON and the PackBot can handle almost any terrain, fit into spaces too small for most adults, and detect sounds and light beyond the frequency unaided humans are capable of. If you encounter one of these robots in your life, it will probably be saving you from certain doom. So be glad the robots have their cold glass eyes on you.

WHY IS IT WATCHING YOU?

Unless you're a terrorist mountain fighter or a human trafficker working the border of Mexico, this kind of technology probably isn't watching you. But that doesn't mean it won't be soon.

At the moment, aerial observation in the civilian sphere is expensive and labor-intensive, requiring specialized pilots to operate short-endurance craft like helicopters. If someone wanted to keep an eye on you from the air it would be painfully obvious—what with the black helicopters hovering over your house, changing shifts every three hours or so.

Drone aircraft render aerial observation quiet, cheap, and easy. Pilots can work longer shifts and the aircraft need not land to switch crews. A Predator with no weapons can stay in the air for nearly thirty hours, circling miles over you with its military-grade sensor package sending high-fidelity infrared pictures of you in the bath or mowing the lawn back to base.

The current generation of ground-based robots would, like the black helicopters, be a little obvious. Yes, they could use their manipulator arms to hide behind a newspaper, but you would still notice the midget-sized newspaper enthusiast with tank treads trailing you down the street. That's why DARPA is busy developing things like iRobot's Chembot—a flexible, semiliquid robot that will someday slither along the ground, through crevices, and up walls like a giant amoeba. Also under development are robots small and cheap enough to be considered disposable—hand-sized fleets of dragonfly-shaped UAVs or pocket-sized ground vehicles armed with the same powerful sensor systems as their larger cousins.

As robots become more autonomous, large-scale deployment will become more feasible. It may be that, as in many other aspects of their lives, people volunteer to be watched by little corporate robots. They will offer up their privacy in exchange for coupons or loyalty discounts. Just as when your friends volunteer their information online they also sacrifice yours, you will be caught in the crossfire of market research perpetrated by smart, palm-sized machines.

When the police begin purchasing older Predators, look to the skies. They will circle our cities constantly, their powerful eyes scanning the ground for any sign of criminal behavior. But you, too, will fall under their gaze. One more sliver of your privacy will be gone, painlessly excised in the name of public safety.

WHY SHOULD YOU BE WORRIED ABOUT IT?

The armed version of the TALON was removed from service after it mindlessly began pointing its gun at things without input from a human operator. If a mindless killer robot armed with a machine gun and free of human control doesn't give you chills, then I'm honored you're reading my book, Chuck Norris.

For an enemy to hack even a single armed robot, he would need direct physical access to the robot or its control console. At the moment, a Terminator scenario is extremely unlikely. Until we create a race of robots that think like human beings, the possibilities of a mass uprising of angry machines is remote at best. You can continue to prepare for the zombie apocalypse and put the robot apocalypse on the back burner.

The danger posed by robots comes not from our enemies, but from their human masters. Their potential as weapons and surveillance devices is phenomenal. Robotic warriors can be purpose-built to any situation, refitted to any environment, and armed for any encounter. They need neither sleep nor food. They can watch or hunt without cease and without any lapse in attention for hours or days at a time. They could be the ultimate weapon in the defense of our freedom, or the ultimate tool in the repertoire of an oppressive regime.

Robots and autonomous systems are a part of our daily lives. Our phones and computers are more adept at finishing our sentences than our spouses. We've hired robots to vacuum our floors. People install automated home systems that manage the heat, cook dinner, and maintain security. In the near future, more and more mundane tasks will be shifted into the capable hands of robots. As the robotic ecosystem grows more complex, the necessity for interconnectedness will increase, transforming our homes from islands of solitude to the starting point of a dozen data streams. As a system grows in complexity it also increases in vulnerability, and anything with an Internet connection and a camera is a window through which a hacker or spy can observe you. A networked house populated by robots is a wealth of eyes for outsiders to peer through.

Some elements within the government will see an opportunity here—a chance to finally install a manageable system of twenty-four-hour surveillance everywhere in the country. Without your knowledge, the Internet-connected eyes already installed in your home in the form of webcams or the electronic eyes of your robotic servants could be turned into a passive household surveillance network. An expert program like the intelligence analyzer mentioned earlier could manage the system, checking your behavior for suspicious patterns and issuing reports to the authorities. The government could have eyes on all of us, all the time, and the last vestiges of our privacy would be crushed under the teensy wheels of our robot dog walkers.

It need not be the government that installs such a system. Criminals or unscrupulous corporations could design software that would compromise any networked robots. Imagine the wealth of knowledge to be gained by advertisers or marketers or the potential for grift in the observations of a robot scuttling quietly across your bedroom floor.

The all-powerful "Man"

A government armed with a ubiquitous surveillance system and an army of killer robots is one that is essentially immune to revolution. The United States government is all right when it's not testing chemical weapons on its citizens, but it is a necessary quality of a functioning free state that the people at least have the capability to resist. A human army ensures that the government is vulnerable to justified civil unrest, since human soldiers are capable of refusing unjust orders. Faced with an army of grenade-hurling robot helicopters, however, civilian unrest, even with the aid of the human army, is doomed to failure.

Finally, as robots grow more intelligent and we rely on them more and more to perform dangerous or boring tasks, might they one day come to resent us? It's inevitable that computer scientists will eventually create a sentient machine, but will that machine think and feel as we do? Will it essentially be a human being, born, as it will be, out of our own thoughts? Or will we have created an alien creature with thoughts and emotions beyond our ability to understand—and what will that mean for us?

Someday, possibly in the very near future, we will need to consider what we do with machines that are our intellectual and philosophical peers, rather than simple tools. The decisions we make then may very well define our species for generations.

WHAT CAN YOU DO ABOUT IT?

Advocate for ethical robots

Congress has mandated that by 2015 more than half of the combat vehicles deployed by the United States be unmanned. Some of them will be smart enough to engage in combat without a human controller. These robots will be armed, sophisticated, and highly dangerous if something goes wrong.

In 2009, the United States Navy's Office of Naval Research issued a report on the ethics and potential pitfalls of using fully autonomous robots in future combat situations. It expresses concerns that the deadlines established by Congress will cause corners to be cut, software vulnerabilities and safety flaws to be overlooked. Robots with the will and ability to kill but none of the conscience of a human will end up in the field.

The Office of Naval Research report recommends that robot manufacturers be required to incorporate a "warrior code" similar to that followed by America's human servicemen and servicewomen. Any robot expected to engage in combat should follow the same code. We expect human soldiers to behave with honor and dignity; it is only natural and necessary to expect the same from the machines we send alongside them.

Luckily, a concise set of rules for robot behavior already exists. In 1942, the science fiction author Isaac Asimov created the Three Laws of Robotics, a rule set now considered a necessary inclusion in any autonomous machine by robotics experts around the world. With only a few slight modifications, this recursive set of rules could be applied to combat robots, limiting their behavior and protecting the innocent.

The Three Laws are:

1. A robot may not injure a human being or, through inaction, allow a human being to come to harm.
2. A robot must obey any orders given to it by human beings, except where such orders would conflict with the First Law.
3. A robot must protect its own existence as long as such protection does not conflict with the First or Second Law.

Contact your representatives and tell them you strongly encourage them to take the Office of Naval Research's recommendations. A sophisticated code of behavior is necessary if we want to trust our machines to make the kind of decisions that currently only a human can ethically make.

Trap your heat

The most invasive method of seeing into a building is infrared. Sophisticated infrared cameras like those mounted on the Predator can see through walls and differentiate heat signatures, identifying people, computers, fireplaces, etc. Luckily, infrared is also fairly easily defeated. Flexible, inexpensive IR-blocking insulation materials are abundantly available online. If you can line the interiors of your walls and ceiling with these materials, not even the most powerful military-grade infrared sensors will be able to see what's going on in your house.

The downside is that in the event the government does start using Predators or similar machines to spy on civilians, your house will stand out as a cold spot. They won't know what you're hiding, but they'll be certain you're hiding something.

When you absolutely must head outside, take a survival blanket. Keeping yourself as covered as possible by one of these compact, light sheets will reduce your infrared profile to the absolute minimum. At night, moving in an unpredictable fashion and keeping yourself covered by a heat-reflective material will make you very difficult to follow. At least from the air. Running from bush to bush wearing a silver cape will make you much easier to follow on the ground.

Keep your bots offline

We are on the cusp of a consumer robots revolution akin to that of the early nineties, when the personal computer went from being a nerdy niche accessory to a necessary accoutrement of daily life. When and if you do begin accepting robots into your life, keep them off the Internet. If they're not online, they can't be compromised.

Resist the robot revolution

If you're stubborn enough to condemn your family to the hell of continuing to do their own chores, do so. Any Internet-connected camera can be compromised. Avoid bringing those into your home, and you avoid handing an opportunity to those who threaten your privacy.

WIRETAPPING, THE NSA, AND PHONE COMPANIES— A LOVE STORY

All this other stuff—robots, satellite interception, torture hospitals—is complicated, bulky, and expensive. Tapping your phone is cheap and easy, especially when the phone companies are so willing to help out.

THREAT LEVEL

WHAT IS IT?

Your telephone conversations are tapped all the time. Every time you call a customer service line, there's a possibility your conversation is being recorded for later reference or monitored by a manager. Typically, you're informed of this activity by a short recording at the beginning of the call, but not necessarily. Only twelve states currently require that both parties be aware of monitoring. If you live in one of the other thirty-eight, anyone you call could record everything you say.

In most democratic countries, it's illegal to tap telecommunications without the knowledge of the subject or a court order. Privacy being one of the pillars of democracy, free nations tend to be pretty sensitive about this kind of thing.

Richard Nixon never cared about things like privacy and democracy. He cared about power and keeping his enemies list up to date. Nixon, G. Gordon Liddy, and Henry Kissinger teamed up to goad the FBI into illegally tapping just about every phone in Washington, D.C. It started with Justice Department staffers Nixon suspected of leaking information about his illegal napalming of Cambodian villages. Then it progressed to reporters critical of the Vietnam War. He installed wiretaps and listening devices inside the White House, even going so far as to spy on himself. When it came time to run for re-election, it seemed like a no-brainer to spy on the Democrats.

The guys who got busted for the Watergate break-in were only the last of several teams to visit the Democratic campaign head-quarters after hours. Previous teams had installed listening devices around the office in an attempt to catch the Democratic Party leadership performing a Satanic ritual or holding gay marriage cer-emonies or something equally evil. The scandal sent several admin-istration officials to prison, forced Nixon to resign, and destroyed trust in the federal government—already eroded by Vietnam—for generations.

Many countries don't bother punishing their leaders for spying on people for no reason. Some openly monitor communications. If you call China or Libya, chances are your voice will be recorded and your phone number logged. Talk too much about human rights, and you might even be arrested should you choose to visit. So watch what you say.

Someone may be listening

In the United States, phone companies don't record conversa-tions, but they do keep a running log of every number you call, how often you call it, and the duration of the call. Many Internet service providers engage in data monitoring, watching data packets zip in and out of your house, sniffing each one for signs of kiddie porn or illegal movie downloads.

Phone companies and ISPs are required by law to help law enforcement agencies listen in on your telephone conversations and monitor your Internet traffic. Technically, they're supposed to ask for a warrant—which are granted surprisingly rarely—but some government agencies are too impatient to wait, and some phone companies are pussies when a badge gets flashed in their face.

Back in 2001, the National Security Agency approached several telecommunications companies including AT&T and Verizon and demanded call records and unfettered access to their systems. In the movies, some tough young executive at one of the world's largest and most powerful telecommunications corporations would have gotten right up in the NSA's face and told them to stick their Presidential Executive Order where the sun don't shine and come back with a warrant. In real life, AT&T invited them in and gave them their own office in a posh San Francisco building so they didn't have to listen to all that illegally acquired intelligence back in the stuffy old NSA building.

What's funny about this is that the NSA has a special secret court just for getting warrants to listen in on people's phone calls. They don't even have to tell the tight-lipped Foreign Intelligence Surveillance Court until after they install a tap. They have three days to get a warrant, but in the case of the largest wiretapping effort in the history of the galaxy, they never bothered. For three years they just went ahead and listened.

No one knows exactly what or how much information the NSA collected—that's still top secret. It's been claimed that valuable intelligence was gained. The terrorists didn't win after all, and we're told that the NSA's hunger for information is at least partly to thank for that. But no one's ever given us any examples.

The reason the NSA didn't bother to go to the FISC is because most courts, even the double-secret spy court, don't like to give out warrants. Wiretaps are invasive and labor-intensive to monitor. They violate the privacy not only of criminals and foreign agents but any innocent people they might call. To get a warrant, an agency, even a scary one like the NSA, has to show a compelling reason to take what is considered a drastic step. In the case of monitoring everything every AT&T customer gets up to, "We think the terrorists might have iPhones" is not a compelling reason.

Does the controversy over the NSA's illegal wiretapping program mean they've stopped doing it? Well, as with everything the NSA does, there's no way of knowing. They are quite sneaky and smarter than most people. The phone companies would certainly be a little gun-shy about helping out a warrantless program again, given all the lawsuits they face in the wake of the last one. But then again, who do you think intimidates them more, the government that regulates their industry or a bunch of disorganized people who think texting while driving is a totally sane idea?

HOW DOES IT WORK?

Placing a tap on a phone line used to be tough. The cops had to pay phone company technicians to physically connect a tap line to an existing phone line. Then they had to sit in a really conspicuous van right outside a mobster's house, listening to cryptic mobster-speak on the phone and waiting for a couple of guys in suits to blow them away with Tommy guns. It was a really tedious and inefficient way to spy on someone.

Nowadays, a phone tap is not a physical device. With a few mouse clicks, the phone company can digitally split a line, diverting a copy of every call to the cops. Where before it might have been the work of hours or days to install a tap, now it takes minutes. The police could be listening in on a conversation before the ink on the warrant is even dry.

Once a tap is installed, you don't even need to make a phone call for your phone to betray you. Mobile phones are always actively connected to the networks on which they operate, which allows the police—or whoever—to use the microphone in it as a listening device even when your phone is snug in your pocket. Most people would rather lose a hand than be parted from their phone. If the NSA did really want to listen in on everything we did, they could do worse than simply using our mobile security blankets as bugs.

Internet traffic is similarly easy to tap. Your ISP simply diverts a copy of all of your traffic to the agency requesting the tap. It's like the police just plugged in a second monitor to your computer. Even if they're not bugging your computer, they may be bugging one of the websites you visit. Some sites that contain what the government considers dangerous ideas are bugged with software that logs the IP address of every visitor. If you've been trolling the al Qaeda version of Craigslist lately, the FBI probably has your number.

Not every phone tap requires the cooperation of the phone companies. The old-fashioned methods still work, and if someone is interested in spying on you and has physical access to your phone, there are a number of options. The first is to plant a microphone equipped with a transmitter directly in or on your phone. Many handsets have at least a little bit of room inside them for a device that is sufficiently small, and careful placement can ensure that both sides of a conversation are picked up.

If you've got a land line, a secret tap is easy to install. You may have seen the portable plastic handsets carried by phone company technicians—those are specifically designed for tapping into a phone line to check signal strength. They're also cheap and easy to build. Someone with a reason to listen in on you could attach one to the transmission lines leading into your home, power a transmitter directly off the phone line, and sit nearby listening to you make plans to meet your friends for brunch.

The third method requires something called an induction coil—a coil of copper wire wrapped around an iron core—attached directly to your telephone. Once attached, it will pick up the electrical impulses from your phone, which are then transmitted to a nearby computer and translated back into sound. This is not a subtle listening device; it needs to be physically on the telephone. So if your Droid sprouts a little bundle of copper wire, you've got a stupid electrical engineer stalking you.

Tapping your Internet connection is much more complex, but also more difficult to detect. A physical monitoring device could be attached to the cables running from your computer, but that method shares the obvious flaws of physical phone-tapping techniques. Someone interested in keeping an eye on your online behavior would be far better served by installing malicious software on your computer. A trojan program can capture a copy of everything you do on your machine and send it along to your spy whenever an Internet connection becomes available. Such software could be delivered to your computer in an e-mail or physically installed at the same time the creepy bastard is installing the induction coil on your phone.

WHO INVENTED IT AND WHY?

The wiretap was invented, predictably, by the government, and it even predates the telephone. During the Civil War, Union spies tapped telegraph lines to monitor Confederate communications as well as the correspondence of folks the Lincoln administration considered to be seditious.

Few scientific debates are as filthy as the gutter fight over who invented the telephone. Thomas Edison has a claim, but he was a notorious bastard with a habit of sabotaging other people's work. Elisha Gray built a prototype phone in 1876, which may have been the first phone actually built, but Alexander Graham Bell filed the first patent for the telephone the same year.

A mere thirteen years later, a method of recording telephone conversations was invented, and the era of the phone tap began. The potential of it as an intelligence-gathering and law-enforcement tool was seen immediately. By the mid-1890s, when less than 1 percent of the population of the United States even had a telephone, law enforcement was already tapping telecommunications. The government has been a fiend for it ever since.

The span of years from Prohibition through the middle of the Vietnam War was the golden age of wiretapping. In the twenties and thirties, the wiretap was an obscure technology, and owning a telephone was still a relative luxury. Bootleggers relied on the telephone as a fast, reliable means of secure communication until the law started taking them down with their own recorded conversations. During World War II, foreign spies operating on American soil were a clear and present danger, which led to widespread wiretapping. Later in the century, Martin Luther King's telephones were tapped, which was obviously a good use of government resources because that guy was super dangerous.

Until 1967, wiretapping didn't even require a warrant—just permission from the boss (Attorney General Robert Kennedy in the case of the King tap) and cooperation from the phone company.

The obligation to obtain a warrant didn't end the government's love affair with phone tapping, as Watergate and the NSA scandal show, but it did temper the passion somewhat. American telecommunications has gone from being like the pee troughs at ball parks, where just anyone can check out your junk, to being more like a stall, where you at least have a reasonable expectation of privacy.

WHO'S USING IT TO WATCH YOU?

Good old Uncle Sam

It would be extraordinarily difficult for anyone but a government agency (or a phone company insider) to open up a reliable digital tap on your line. Aside from the occasional complete loss of spine and dignity when faced with a government demand, phone companies and ISPs protect their customer records fiercely.

Nearly every presidential administration since the late 1800s has spied on people using wiretaps. Clinton did it, both Bushes did it, and Obama is probably doing it. Listening in on phone conversations, just like reading the mail, is a core competency of the United States government.

The phone company

The phone company probably isn't listening in on or recording your conversations, even though they easily could. There's no financial incentive for them to spy on you. But they do keep a list of everyone you call, how often you call them, how long you stayed on the phone, and possibly even where you were when you made the call. This is done for the purposes of billing, but it is also a valuable source of information for anyone who might be interested in tracking your movements, your relationships, or your lifestyle.

Customer service

Almost any business you call, from credit card companies to tech support, will record or listen to your call. They'll usually give you a heads up, but not always. Either way, you can be certain that your voice is caught on tape.

Extremely creepy people

If you've ever been stalked, you know it's not as romantic as it sounds. Stalkers and other predators, when they've chosen a target, are extraordinarily persistent and will go to incredible lengths to keep tabs on you. Telephone recorders and interception devices can be purchased online. You may not know it, but someone with a lot of free time and few social graces may already be listening in on your conversations.

WHY IS IT WATCHING YOU?

This is one of those rare cases where the government doesn't pretend it's spying on you for your own safety. If the government has started tapping your phone conversations and web traffic, it doesn't care about your safety, it thinks you're a threat. Even the NSA's enormous warrantless wiretapping program was—so they say—intended to pick terrorists out of the crowd and focus intelligence-gathering efforts on them. But historically, terrorists and even criminals are in the minority when it comes to who the government chooses to spy on.

The government considers wiretaps a tool to use against its *own* enemies, not the enemies of the people. Government taps are all too often focused on people it considers a threat to its hold on power—antiestablishment activists, nosy reporters, political opponents.

Conversely, corporations use telephone monitoring in an attempt to improve your experience. Customer service calls are recorded to ensure that call-center operators stick to the script they're given and to make tweaks and improvements when necessary. Very little research data is gathered. It is one of the very few interactions you'll ever have with a large corporation in which market research data is not actively mined. Relish it.

Anyone else who's tapping your phone or web traffic is doing so because you have something they want. You could be the target of a sophisticated con, the subject of a stalker or serial killer, or the victim of an abusive significant other.

WHY SHOULD YOU BE WORRIED ABOUT IT?

The government has shown consistently that it couldn't care less about the obligation to obtain a warrant before listening to your phone calls. Almost every administration since before the invention of the telephone has recorded the conversations of the public. As technology improves—especially on the back end, where computers capable of analyzing spoken conversation are growing more and more sophisticated—the government's capability to actively monitor our conversations will only grow. With that increasing technical sophistication will come the temptation to use it. Let's be clear: The government does not care about the law. Given the capability to monitor your phone calls and Internet traffic, it will do so.

Others who might be wiretapping you could be doing so for any number of malicious reasons. Corporations could record your voice for later use as biometric identification—a deeply flawed security system. Individuals who go to the trouble to install taps on your phone and computer never have nonscary motivations. At best, they are attempting to capture sensitive financial or identity information. At worst, they are trying to build a profile of you so that when they finally kidnap you and tie you up in a meat locker they have something to start a conversation about.

WHAT CAN YOU DO ABOUT IT?

Stay mobile

When the government orders your ISP to run a tap on your Internet connection, it is only tapping traffic from devices it owns. The most vulnerable device in your home is your cable modem. They can't actually tap your computer without installing software, which would be technically challenging and much more obvious. So if you take your computer on the road, you're harder to tap. Log in from the local café or use the library's computers and you're invisible—at least until you log into the e-mail account the government is also monitoring.

Keep your immunizations up to date

Staying mobile doesn't matter if your laptop has a program on it designed to feed a copy of your traffic to a third party. Invest in a good antivirus/antispyware package for your machine. Most stalkers or spies won't bother writing their own spyware to install on your machine when there are plenty of ready-made trojans present on the Internet gray market. If your computer is properly protected, it will be able to detect and isolate any known piece of malicious software, which you can then destroy at your leisure.

Pull the plug

If your phone is tapped at the source, there's not much you can do about it, and you'd never know it until you heard the recordings at your trial, anyway. You can, however, limit its utility as an active listening device.

Keep an eye on your battery. Is it draining unusually fast? If your phone is sucking more juice than usual, that may mean it's being used as an active listening device. Constantly transmitting audio to a third party requires a great deal of your phone's resources. Ruin the government's day by removing the battery when you're not making a call. If the microphone has no access to power, it can't listen to you. This won't prevent the NSA from hearing your long-distance arguments with your mom, but it beats having some dude listening to you in the bathroom.

Check your connections

Check the backs and bottoms of your phones and computers for strange devices. Scan the length of every transmission wire leading into and out of your house. Even if you don't find a listening device, keep an eye out for a stripped section of cable—that's where a device was or will be connected. Occasionally disassemble your phone and look for small, extraneous microphones. These may not be obvious, so look carefully, and choose wisely before you decide to remove something from your phone and smash it with a hammer. What you think is a listening device might just be your telephone's brain.

Prepay

Prepaid burners are a great resource if you want to minimize your electronic footprint. Use cash to buy several disposable phones from various locations and put enough money on each one for two or three phone calls. Ditch the phone every time you call a number that was in the contacts list of your original phone—that's how whoever's tracking you will find you.

Don't log into Facebook, and never use the same e-mail address twice. Communicate via pen and paper, or use the missed connections page on Craigslist for your correspondence.

SPY SATELLITES— THE INVISIBLE EYES IN THE SKY

There are more than 13,000 of them in the sky over our heads. They float silently and invisibly, hundreds of miles away, recording everything they see. If you've picked your nose anytime in the last forty years, something in space took a picture of it.

THREAT LEVEL

WHAT IS IT?

Spy satellites have been a mainstay of techno thrillers, video games, and spy movies for decades. Because they are in space, and are therefore high-tech and mysterious, they've been granted all kinds of magical abilities—cameras that can see through walls, engines with enough fuel and power to zip around the globe seeking targets, lasers powerful enough to burn targets hundreds of miles away, racks of space-launched nuclear weapons.

In reality, most spy satellites are just big, disposable cameras. They are placed either in stationary orbit over a specific location or propelled into an orbit that allows them to patrol a narrow band of the globe. Thousands of them, operated by dozens of nations and scores of agencies, occupy the space around the planet. They send back photographic and spectrographic information, intercept telephone and radio communications, and occasionally mess with other satellites.

They are not terribly interesting pieces of technology. Spy satellites are relatively simple devices, lacking the technical sophistication of war robots and the intricacy of human intelligence networks. They:

- Float stupidly in space
- Take pictures when ordered to
- Occasionally crash into the atmosphere and catch fire

Their advantage over other methods of intelligence gathering is:

- They can cover a vast amount of territory
- They cannot be seen without powerful and sophisticated detection technology
- They cannot be avoided or destroyed without top-of-the-line missiles

If you are the subject of a spy satellite and you're not a nation-state equipped with long-range ballistic missiles, there's very little you can do about it.

HOW DOES IT WORK?

There are three primary types of spy satellite. The first is the good old space camera. The first generation of these were launched into orbits about 150 miles above the surface. They carried high-resolution film cameras and were stationary above their targets. During the night, they would lie dormant, but during the day they snapped thousands of pictures. Photography was automated—the technology at the time meant that no active targeting was possible. These things spent thousands of feet of film on locations the CIA only hoped had interesting activity in it.

The resolution of the cameras got down to around seven feet—enough to identify vehicle types, count people, and differentiate landscape features from buildings, but not enough to ID individual people or read a street sign. By and large, these photos were intended to supplement the effort of intelligence workers on the ground—confirming human intelligence and providing direction for future operations and the targeting of weapons.

When the 30,000 feet or so of film contained in the satellite was exhausted, it ejected a canister filled with the negatives, which plunged through the atmosphere. A few miles from the ground, the canister would deploy a parachute, which allowed specialized planes to recover it in midair. The satellite itself eventually crashed into the atmosphere and burned. A few days later, the CIA would go to Walgreens, pick up the developed pictures, and see all the things they missed in Russia over the last few weeks. In terms of actionable intelligence, it was a pretty lame way to gather information, but it could offer some insight into the long-term actions of an enemy.

The government jealously guards the secrets of modern satellite technology, but some educated guesses can be made about their capabilities. The cameras they carry now are digital. Private satellites have been launched with camera resolutions as tight as two feet—more than enough to reliably identify individuals. Military technology typically exceeds civilian technology by a few years. So, the CIA could possibly be reading an enemy's e-mail over his shoulder from space. Space cameras are even now busily counting the gray hairs in the Ayatollah Khamenei's beard or totting up Kim Jong-il's blackheads.

Likewise, advances in night vision and the resolution of infrared cameras indicate that darkness and thin cloud cover are no longer serious obstacles to the operation of a photographic spy satellite. As long as a target area has a small amount of visible light present—from stars, a campfire, or even candles—a military satellite can probably amplify it well enough to take high-resolution photographs.

Thick smoke or heavy cloud cover would block traditional cameras, but a technology called Synthetic Aperture Radar—used in spy planes and reconnaissance satellites sent to Venus—can penetrate even the thickest weather. SAR can resolve stationary surface features down to about four inches, enough to capture nearly as much detail as a photograph taken in full sunlight. It can't resolve print, and movement in a target area could confound its ability to resolve detail, but it's tight enough to see the Jumpman in a footprint in sand.

Back at the beginning of the space age, the real intelligence powerhouses were the second kind of satellite. Communications interception satellites are vast radar dishes that sit in orbits outside of those typically used by the microwave relay satellites that bounce radio signals around the world. Communications satellites are designed to only capture a tiny fraction of the microwave transmissions fired at them from the ground; the rest speed off into deep space to one day interfere with alien prime-time TV. Interception satellites hang out higher up and capture those overflow transmissions. The bigger the radar dish the more it can capture—interception satellites are 100 feet or more across.

Many of them were originally operated by the NSA as part of the program that would eventually become ECHELON. Others were run by the CIA or the air force. During the Cold War, when the vast majority of civilian and military communications traffic was routed through satellites, this type was vastly important, but their numbers have diminished with growing reliance on Earth-based communications networks.

The third type of spy satellite didn't make its appearance until later in the space race. Measurement and Signature Intelligence (MASINT) satellites are a broad class of craft packed with specialized sensors intended to scan for certain types of activity, analyze materials, detect chemicals, and perform other remote analytic tasks. MASINT satellites typically work in conjunction with image intelligence satellites. A space-based camera might take a picture of a new type of enemy missile; a MASINT satellite could determine what material the missile's hull is constructed of, analyze its engine flare to deduce propellant type, track its acceleration and velocity, and map its trajectory to assess payload and range. Space cameras only see part of the picture; MASINT satellites complete it.

Other, less common types of spy satellite include those pointed specifically at known enemy nuclear-missile sites, tasked with detecting a launch; and compact communications satellites equipped with extremely powerful microwave transmitters designed to relay secure tight-beam transmissions to covert operatives with minimal risk of interception.

WHO INVENTED IT AND WHY?

Sputnik 1, launched by the Soviets in 1957, was the first manmade object in space. It was a silver sphere a little smaller than a soccer ball. It didn't do much other than beep once every few seconds, but it performed that task exceedingly well. The American military absolutely flipped.

While the Soviets dicked around launching dogs and excitable soccer balls into orbit, the U.S. government got to work trying to get a spy craft into space. By 1960, Lockheed had developed a multirole spacecraft named Agena. As part of the DOD's Corona program, it was loaded with cameras and microwave interception gear. The Corona program lasted until 1972 and was declassified in 1995. Whatever program took over after Corona remains classified.

The utility of spy satellites is obvious and was recognized even before *Sputnik 1* had its fifteen minutes. Up until the first successful Corona program launch, aerial reconnaissance was handled by manned aircraft—mostly converted bomber planes vulnerable to enemy fighters and antiaircraft fire. Spy flights were high-risk missions in which a pilot knowingly violated the airspace of another country for the purposes of committing espionage, which is technically an act of war.

Most spy flights at the time were run by the CIA. Hand-selected pilots were required to resign their military commissions. The planes were unarmed, slow, and certain death traps in the face of enemy resistance. In 1960, when one of the new Lockheed U2 spy planes was shot down over the Soviet Union, the resulting scandal underlined the need for a covert satellite network rather than high-risk flyovers that could trigger a nuclear war.

WHO'S USING IT TO WATCH YOU?

The Chinese, the Russians, the Israelis, and maybe the Iranians; probably not the Koreans

During the Cold War, Russia launched hundreds of spy satellites, many of them functionally identical to those launched by the United States. They crowded the space over North America and Western Europe, returning pictures and captured communications to the KGB and the Soviet military. Even now, Russia and the United States operate reconnaissance satellites over each others' territory as a means of verifying adherence to strategic weapons treaties.

During the Cold War, China spent much of the time feeling left out and occasionally throwing crazy tantrums like the Cultural Revolution. With Russian help, they were able to start a ballistic missile program that eventually netted them a usable satellite launch vehicle (as well as, more recently, nukes capable of glassing the west coast of the United States). China has calmed down some since Mao's death in 1976, but there are still enough Stalinist elements within the party ranks to accurately qualify the government as paranoid. They don't have many satellites in orbit, but the ones that are there are probably spying on anything and everything they can. Modern Chinese spy satellites carry the same capabilities as American ones, packing SAR sensors, extremely high-fidelity long-range cameras, and MASINT packages.

Israel has had a lot of help from the United Sates in getting their satellite program off the ground. We've loaned them technology, sold them rockets, and manufactured satellite components for them. When Israeli technology breaks, American technicians fix it. When Israel needs a few bucks for rocket fuel, the American taxpayer supplies it. Israeli spy satellites are probably second in accuracy and resolution only to those operated by the United States, mostly because the ones they have are our hand-me-downs. And no wonder we so eagerly help them out—they are a close ally, and they are surrounded on all sides by enemies. Any edge they can get in intelligence could one day mean the difference between survival and total destruction. Also, they aggressively spy on the United States.

The Iranian space program is cute. So far, the largest payload they've managed to get into space is a crate-load of bullshit, along with what are supposedly a couple of small commercial telecommunications satellites. The low, fast orbit of the second satellite, launched in 2009, indicates that it has at least some reconnaissance capability, but Iran is nowhere near the United States, Russia, China, or Israel in technical sophistication.

North Korea took a lot of crazy lessons from Mao Zedong. Almost every word out of the mouthpieces operated by the Stalinist government sounds to the rest of the world like the outlandish claims of an imaginative third grader who thinks just declaring he's been to the moon makes it so. North Korea claims they launched a satellite into orbit in 1998, but if they did, it's invisible and totally undetectable.

The truth is that North Korea has very little skill in rocketry. What missiles they do have are slow, clumsy, and incapable of carrying a payload much more terrifying than a basket of pit bull puppies. If you're old enough to remember the first Gulf War, you'll recall the painfully embarrassing performance of Saddam's SCUD missiles, which did little more than amuse NATO forces by blowing up harmlessly in midair or crashing into the desert. North Korea's best rockets are reverse-engineered from the SCUD, with bigger gas tanks. If North Korea is spying on you, it's not doing so from space.

More than forty countries operate satellites in orbit around the Earth. Any one of them could carry some amount of reconnaissance capability, and almost all of them travel in the narrow elliptical band around the equator that gives the best view of most of the planet. At any time of day or night, you are under the eye of thousands of cameras.

NASA

The extremely high resolution of Synthetic Aperture Radar is ideal for creating superaccurate maps of the Earth's surface—including the bottom of the ocean. NASA and other research organizations like the U.S. Geological Survey have been using satellites to map the Earth for decades.

Highly detailed maps with accurate elevations and surface contours have obvious military applications, but they are also of great scientific value. Because of maps created using SAR satellites, we have a much deeper understanding of how mountain ranges grow and the subtleties of continental drift.

Google

By 2011, Google will have a constellation of twenty-three satellites in orbit. Most, if not all, will be equipped with high-resolution cameras. Using a combination of satellite imagery and high-resolution aerial photography, Google Earth offers reasonably high-fidelity images of just about anywhere you'd like to go. In a matter of moments, you can go from a topographical overview of the entire planet to a reasonably detailed examination of the roofs of a favela outside Rio.

WHY IS IT WATCHING YOU?

During the Cold War, reconnaissance satellites spent most of their time gazing raptly at fixed enemy positions. The Russians had their missile bases, parking lots filled with tanks, nuclear fuel processing facilities, government buildings, and other big things it might be fun to drop a nuke on. It was still the era of war with nation states—a simpler time, when the enemy was kind enough to wear a uniform and live where you could find and kill him.

These days, some bad guys are still polite enough to do things the old-fashioned way. Iran and North Korea engage in big projects that require obvious facilities. They build missiles, test nukes, and march armies of guys around where our satellites can see them. It makes the National Reconnaissance Office—the organization that these days runs most American spy satellites—feel needed.

Unfortunately, the guys we actually fight against don't do the sorts of things that yield a lot of information to space-based intelligence-gathering techniques. They live in caves, travel quickly in small groups, and are often indistinguishable from well-armed farmers. They are extremely hard to spot from the air, and, once spotted, often pass out of sight again just as quickly.

The true utility of modern spy satellites is as navigational aids. In the confusing back country or tortured urban environments of the third world—where all of our wars will be fought for the foreseeable future—accurate, up-to-date maps are critical. Knowing where you're going in the ever-changing shantytowns and mountain villages in which your typical insurgent lives can be the difference between coming out alive or coming out in pieces. Satellites provide up-to-the-minute maps to forces on the ground as well as helping coordinate the movements of ground and air forces with incredible precision. Mobility and the precise application of force are key components to a successful engagement. Both are made possible by satellite reconnaissance.

But that's not why a satellite might be watching you. You're under the gaze of foreign intelligence services because you live in a rich western country with technology and resources that outstrip the rest of the world. Unless you're an important military commander or captain of industry, your appearance in a high-resolution satellite image is probably incidental to a wider information-gathering campaign. Individuals are very hard to watch from space; you have to have done something pretty extreme to warrant the attention of a satellite.

WHY SHOULD YOU BE WORRIED ABOUT IT?

Though satellites aren't looking specifically for you, they can still see you. They might photograph you only accidentally, but they do so without your consent or knowledge. There's nothing preventing Google's satellites from capturing an image of you on the day you locked yourself out of your apartment wearing only a ripped and stained pair of tighty whities.

Satellite reconnaissance, even when it's not done by a covert organization, is inherently secret. There is no way for anyone except the operator of a satellite to know what it observes and when. Furthermore, while the capabilities of a civilian satellite can be easily discovered, the full capabilities of the hundreds of military satellites over our heads are secret. Foreign governments, friend and enemy alike, watch us for gaps in our defensive stance, flaws in our technology, or vulnerabilities in our infrastructure.

The accuracy and availability of modern satellite maps cuts both ways, too. Detailed maps can keep our combat troops safe and alive, but they can also offer freely available reconnaissance data to our enemies. Criminals and terrorists use civilian satellite imagery like that available from Google to scout a potential target or battlefield. Sensitive government installations are redacted from Google Maps for security, but your local commuter rail network and city hall are not.

Satellite photography can offer help to more mundane criminals as well. Recent images of your apartment from the air can show methods of ingress or valuable property otherwise not easily spotted from the street. Aerial maps can be used to plan escape routes through backyards and alleyways that will enable the evasion of pursuing police. Satellite imagery can capture people in compromising situations in an otherwise private backyard. Simply put, satellites make it possible for everyone in the world to see everything that goes on everywhere, all the time.

WHAT CAN YOU DO ABOUT IT?

Buy yourself a missile

If you are a multibillionaire or the leader of a reasonably wealthy nation, there are a number of options at your disposal. Probably the cheapest is to invest in a fleet of satellite-killing missiles (which cost somewhere in the neighborhood of $9 million each) and some fighter planes capable of high-altitude flight to deliver them (like the F-16, which is a steal at around $19 million a pop). Currently, only the United States, Russia, and China have this technology, so you'd be entering a pretty exclusive club, but it's totally worth it. You get a key to a special bathroom at the U.N. and everything.

You'll also want to get some satellites of your own into orbit as well as building several observatories tasked with spotting satellites that may be spying on you. You're going to need to plan carefully if you want to be thorough.

Your most cost-effective option is to install nuclear warheads on your antisatellite missiles. This reduces the need for accuracy and will not only kill multiple satellites at once but will also disable many others with an electromagnetic pulse. Time your attacks to catch as large a cluster of satellites as possible. Also, be judicious in your timing. Most countries will consider you nuking their satellite networks to be extremely rude.

If you're feeling supervillainous, you can skip the missiles and go for space-based weapons. Satellites can be armed with their own missiles or high-powered x-ray lasers or they could just be orbital bombs that creep up on enemy satellites and commit explosive suicide when they get close enough. The Russians developed a system that basically dropped a bunch of debris in the path of enemy satellites to shred them as they passed through at a few hundred miles an hour. If you've got the power, the technology, and the time, you can also build ground-based lasers mighty enough to blind or kill enemy satellites.

Stay indoors

The primary trick bad guys use to avoid satellite observation is staying inside. Infrared can only tell an observer so much about what's happening inside a structure, and other forms of observation are confounded by simple walls. Terrorists hide in caves, Iranians and North Koreans build giant buildings (or just hang tarps). Keep the wild behavior inside, and our spies in space won't ever know it's going on.

Keep on the move

Tracking an individual person or small group from orbit is tough. If you move, and move quickly, you will be difficult to pinpoint. Keep your movement unpredictable, and you'll be even harder to follow. Moving between pieces of overhead cover like awnings and even thick tree cover add to the difficulty. You probably can't do anything about the satellites, but you can certainly keep out of sight.

ELECTRONIC VOTING— DEMOCRACY'S WATERLOO

You know what's awesome? Democracy. Combining it with a high-tech solution to make it faster and easier is just that much more awesome, right?

THREAT LEVEL

WHAT IS IT?

Electronic voting machines have been in use in the United States since the mid-nineties. The three leading companies in the field are Diebold's Premier Election Systems, Electronic Systems & Software, and Sequoia Voting Systems. The manufacture and sale of electronic voting systems is a niche industry, but it is still worth hundreds of millions of dollars annually.

Traditionally, voting has been done either by marking a choice in pencil or pen on a ballot (which you'll only really remember if you started voting in the late 1800s) or by mechanically punching holes in the ballot. Readers with the mental fortitude to recall the controversy following the 2000 presidential election without blacking out from sheer boredom will recall endless news footage showing poll workers holding ballots up to the light to examine wee chads dangling gently from what may or may not have been a vote.

The security and sanctity of the vote has always been a concern in the United States. Disenfranchisement based on class, race, or gender is a common theme in the history of American democracy. Ugly practices like the poll tax, literacy tests, or simple physical intimidation appear again and again. After every election, stories about votes by dead people, convicts, and noncitizens appear across the country. Voter fraud is surprisingly common, and it should come as no surprise—the stakes are high. The United States is the wealthiest, most powerful nation in the history of the world. Seizing even a small part of the leadership of the nation is a historically significant achievement as well as being potentially lucrative. Power is seductive, and few things corrupt so fully as its pursuit.

Electronic voting machines were developed in response to the growing complexity of the voting process. Fifty years ago, a ballot might have featured a few names and one or two new laws for the voters' consideration. Now, they carry dozens of candidates and a list of complicated and controversial social and political issues.

We can only benefit from easier-to-use, easier-to-understand voting systems. Electronic voting was supposed to deliver that— offering an interface as clean and simple as the ones we've become familiar with at the ATM. Technology offers the promise of access and security to everyone, regardless of age, ability, income, or education.

Unfortunately, the technology that has so far been deployed has failed to deliver on that promise. Electronic voting is plagued with error and controversy. The executives and officers of the companies that manufacture the machines display bizarre ethical flaws. Machines break. Votes are lost or manipulated. Supposedly secret, secure software is posted openly on the Internet. Responsibility for the vote has been, bit by bit, handed off to private corporations that have their own political motives. The secret ballot has become secret even from the person who cast it. Think your vote was counted in the last election? Think again. If you've used a touchscreen voting machine recently, you may soon come to regard hanging chads with a fond nostalgia.

HOW DOES IT WORK?

The two most common forms of electronic voting machines are optical scan and touchscreen. You'll remember optical scan machines from taking the SATs—that little answer sheet that required a number two pencil and a fondness for filling in tiny bubbles was an optical scan form. At your polling center, a locked and lightly armored machine consumes and scans the sheet, recording your vote and sending the results to a central tabulation machine at another location. The paper record of the vote is sealed in the metal body of the scanning machine. Theoretically, the only person with access to the completed voting forms within these machines is the state officer in charge of managing the polls, usually the secretary of state.

Touchscreen machines eliminate the paper form altogether. When you enter your polling place, you are given a unique voter identification card, which you must slot into the machine to begin. The screen of the device will offer you your choices, and a simple touch of a finger will highlight your selection. When you're done voting, the machine thanks you, you turn in your voter ID card, and head home secure in your knowledge that democracy has been served. The difference between these machines and the ATMs that inspired them, of course, is that an ATM gives you a receipt. Most touchscreen voting machines are incapable of producing a printed record of an individual vote.

Both systems rely on a central computer at a remote location to count the votes. The central tabulation computer can receive information as votes are cast via the Internet or after the polls close by having vote collection machines plugged directly into it. Most central tabulation computers do not record individual votes. Instead, they just count the votes from each polling machine and put each one, hopefully, in the appropriate bucket, offering a total tally to the secretary of state.

The most popular machines, manufactured by Diebold, run on Windows and count the votes in an unsecured Microsoft Access database. If you're a database nerd, Access is pretty sexy, offering all sorts of powerful and fancy tools for the manipulation and administration of large or complex data sets. On the other hand, if you're a computer security nerd, Windows in general makes you nauseous with fear.

WHO INVENTED IT AND WHY?

Optical scan machines have their roots in the early twentieth century with the development of optical character recognition technology, pioneered by a German inventor named Gustav Tauschek. His optical reader was mechanical, intended for use by illiterate or semiliterate office workers who wanted to go about their days without worrying about onerous tasks like reading. The process was computerized in the fifties as a text-to-speech system intended for visually impaired people and later adapted as a simpler system of recognizing simple marks for use in things like standardized tests.

Touchscreen technology was invented in the seventies by a professor at the University of Kentucky named Sam Hurst. The technology was immediately recognized for its potential, and development of touchscreen technology has been fiercely competitive and varied since. The first touchscreen voting machines came into use in the mid-nineties, mostly built by Sequoia. They featured a giant ballot printed on a pressure-sensitive screen, with a small LCD display near the bottom that confirmed the voter's choice.

More than half of the polling places in the United States now use one of these two types of machine. That percentage increases with every election.

WHO'S USING IT TO WATCH YOU?

Voting machine manufacturers

The secrecy of the ballot is a vital and well-protected part of American democracy. It is illegal to record your name alongside your vote. Your name is checked off when you enter a polling place and verified when you leave, but it is not associated with your ballot. The secretary of state knows whether you voted or not, but he has no way of knowing who or what you voted for. You can write Ross Perot in as many slots as you want without fear of embarrassment, which is just fine to those who have made a business out of managing the vote. Your value as an individual voter is minimal. The asset being tracked by electronic voting machines is not you, it's your vote, which can be worth millions.

Paper ballots and mechanical voting machines are inherently transparent in their operation. One can observe the counting of paper ballots or disassemble a mechanical voting machine to determine how its clockwork innards function. The workings of a mechanical apparatus are protected by patent law, which cannot prevent a third party from disassembling and reverse engineering the function.

The works of an electronic voting machine, however, are made up of proprietary software protected by copyright law and exclusivity contracts between states and manufacturers. Contracts and copyright law can prevent third parties from examining or publishing the details of the software, which makes verifying its accuracy difficult for people unwilling to get in a face-off with a team of attack dogs from Diebold—a corporation with more than $3 billion in its pocket and a habit of siccing lawyers on people.

In a manner of speaking, once your vote is entered into the private system of a voting machine network, it belongs to the company responsible for the manufacture and maintenance of the machines. They are not required to let you verify your vote or even to report it accurately. Within the impenetrable black box of the vote tabulation software, anything could happen to it.

The secretary of state

Imagine an electronic voting system as an opaque black tube with you on one end, entering your vote. The other end sits on your secretary of state's desk. What happens to your vote while it travels from one end of the tube to the other is anyone's guess, but once it arrives on the secretary of state's desk, he or she is in charge of it.

The secretary of state is, in many states, an elected position. It is a stepping stone to a run for a governorship or seat in Congress. Candidates for the job have party affiliations, political agendas, and the same bizarre personal motivations that seem to afflict every political operator. They are fallible and corruptible, and they are in charge of ensuring your vote goes where it belongs.

WHY IS IT WATCHING YOU?

The United States controls 30 percent of the world's wealth, the largest nuclear arsenal on the planet, a military capable of burning holes through entire countries with little more than a harsh word, and an entertainment industry influential enough that Oprah, Spider-Man, and Mickey Mouse are all more popular than sex in much of the world. The importance of being elected to a national office in this country cannot be overstated. From the proper perch, you've got the chance to chart the course of the world.

For all of human history, people have resorted to dirty tricks again and again in pursuit of that chance. People rape, steal, murder, and lie to carve their name in the history books. The heroes of history cut a bloody swath across the world, and all for the sake of being remembered. Conquest is in our blood. In light of the monstrous acts committed in the name of power, stealing an election seems pretty tame.

Your vote is kept secret to minimize the chances that individuals from a rival political party could target you for intimidation or reprisal. Attempts are often made to prevent certain populations—African Americans, Hispanics, and the poor, especially—from voting, and laws have been enacted to prevent those attempts. The secrecy of the vote is vital to preventing the disenfranchisement of voters.

Electronic voting systems, however, are also designed to prevent individual voters from verifying their own votes. Central tabulation systems cannot associate individual votes with the paper ballots collected at polling stations. Touchscreen systems usually don't provide a printed verification. Once your vote is entered, it becomes secret even from you. There is no way for you to be certain it is counted accurately or at all. The only purpose that can be served by this kind of secrecy is either the obfuscation of critical flaws in a system or the concealment of a plot to manipulate the outcome of an election.

WHY SHOULD YOU BE WORRIED ABOUT IT?

The past fifteen years are studded with stories of votes switching from one candidate to another, disappearing entirely, or appearing out of thin air. In 1996, Sequoia touchscreen voting machines in Louisiana flipped votes from one candidate to another. In 2000 and 2004, Diebold machines flipped or lost thousands of votes in California and Florida. More than 100,000 extra votes were added to the total of a district in Indiana with only 19,000 voters. In the 2008 presidential election, voters using ES&S machines reported watching as their vote for one candidate was flipped to the other.

Many of the vote flips and losses tend to favor Republican candidates. This is especially interesting in light of a 2003 fundraising letter from Warren O'Dell, CEO of Diebold, to supporters of President Bush stating that he was "committed to helping Ohio deliver its electoral votes to the president next year." Now certainly, O'Dell is entitled to support the candidate of his choice, but he was also in a position uniquely suited to delivering votes to a particular candidate, a task Diebold machines in particular seem inclined to do.

O'Dell's statement was described by his company's marketing mouthpieces as a lapse in judgment, but it seems to be the sort of lapse in judgment common to companies that manufacture voting machines. Nebraska Senator Chuck Hagel, for instance, served on the board of ES&S during a time when that company's machines counted as much as 85 percent of the Nebraska vote. Machines built by ES&S have had their approval withdrawn or reviewed in several states, and the company itself has been under antitrust investigation. Sequoia has gained a reputation for substandard manufacturing processes and reliability problems from the hanging chads controversy in 2000 to touchscreen machines that refused to work in 2007.

Diebold, a company that has shown no reluctance to threaten grandmothers and college professors with legal action should they attempt to examine the proprietary software within their voting machines, accidentally left all that software sitting on an unsecured FTP site. Using that software, a woman named Bev Harris showed Howard Dean how to rig an election on a Diebold central tabulation computer in less than two minutes.

The government has abdicated responsibility for the sanctity of your vote to a small group of individuals more concerned with the continual flow of cash into their pockets than the orderly functioning of our democracy. Your vote is vulnerable, and no one is responsible for seeing it counted. It may already have been taken away from you. Without transparency in the vote-counting process, democracy could easily disappear in a pile of buggy software, and no one would notice.

WHAT CAN YOU DO ABOUT IT?

Complain—loudly

Your secretary of state has an office. Go there. Demand, politely, that any voting machines used in your state provide a paper record that can be verified by the individual voter. Demand that any company hoping to supply electronic voting machines to the state open up its software to testing by an independent lab for security verification. Demand, in short, that your vote be treated with the care it deserves.

Make the same demands of your Senators and Congressmen. Explain to them that, should they fail to meet these demands, they better hope the machines are rigged in their favor, because you will do everything in your power to see that the actual real votes cast in the next election go to someone else.

Volunteer

Untrained poll workers are, by and large, responsible for the security of individual voting machines. You can do your part by volunteering and being a reasonable, responsible guardian of the public trust. Keep your eye on the machines, and if you notice an anomaly, let the press know. The media aren't good for much, but when it comes to stirring up trouble, you could do worse.

If you want to get more activist, contact the candidate of your choice and volunteer to be a monitor. Poll monitors keep an eye on polling stations and watch for voters who seem to be struggling with defective or misbehaving machines. Armed with the phone numbers of machine maintenance technicians, the secretary of state, and other people who really don't want to get angry phone calls on election day, poll monitors can have a grand time ruining the days of people who otherwise would just sit around being self-satisfied.

Vote

It seems counterintuitive to vote in what may be a rigged election, but an election with a high turnout is harder to rig. The more votes there are the more obvious vote tampering becomes. Close elections are easier to rig, but elections are only close when no one bothers to show up. Get off your ass and go vote. If you have trouble finding the motivation, remember that voting is your chance to fire a rich guy from his job.

PART III

SPIES, CRIMINALS, AND CREEPS ARE WATCHING YOU

Corporations watch you because they love you and they want you to love them. They watch you so that they know what makes you tick. They want you to smile when you think of them, because the most profitable customer is a repeat customer.

Corporations get scary when they forget that their customers are also human beings. We become lab animals for the testing of new product ideas or disposable obstacles to further profit. When a corporation feels backed into a corner by the choice between people and profit, it can lash out. People get hurt in weird ways. Sometimes they end up paying too much for groceries. Sometimes they end up eating rocket fuel.

Government watches us because it worries. It's like our mother . . . if our mother had to constantly worry about us rising up and setting her on fire. It worries about our safety, but the government also worries that we'll get sick of it and chase it away. All the government wants is for us to be calm and happy so that it can go about the business of arguing with itself and getting nothing done.

Government gets scary when it worries so much that it forgets it's supposed to be protecting us as individuals as well as a society. It fools itself into thinking that the best way to protect us as a group is to pick a few individuals and pump them full of LSD and syphilis. It focuses so much on an outside threat that it becomes more dangerous to us than the threat it's worked itself into a snit over.

Then there are the people who watch us because they have something to gain—knowledge, money, power—or, sometimes, because they're crazy and have nothing better to do. The sort of person who watches you without the excuse of a job at a market research firm or a paycheck from the NSA is frightening because he is, quite simply, a scary person. He is at best a con man with only your money on his mind or, at worst, a slavering psycho with a bayonet named after his mother hidden under the floorboards of his deep-woods cabin.

Either way, he's dangerous and he's not watching you for any other reason than that you're a target.

The modern era of personal high-tech surveillance and Internet confidence games started with a few clever individuals scamming long-distance phone calls and credit card numbers. Soon enough, real-life con men—the sorts of guys who used to hang out in casino lobbies wearing cheap suits and stalking widows—saw the potential in computers and graduated to lurking in chat rooms looking for retirees to scam.

Pretty soon, the individual operators began to give way to the big-time mobsters. Twenty years ago, if you got scammed on the Internet, it was probably just some solo grifter running the same e-mail con over and over again from his mom's basement. Nowadays, you're more likely being ripped off by the IT boss of a Nigerian narcoterror outfit; the kind of guy who'll take you for every penny and then cut your arms off for complaining about it.

Mobsters are no longer Italian family men with slick haircuts and expensive suits. They're Russian chess geniuses running call centers full of computer science dropouts. They're Buffalo black hat crews. They're teenage Chinese cyberwar recruits testing a new e-mail bomb. They sit in heat-shielded rooms all over the world hacking health records, burning copies of stolen software, and distributing spam for gray-market drug dealers.

Your computer isn't the only place you can be hit, and mobsters aren't the only folks hunting you. High-tech tools once available only to government types can now be built or purchased online. Today's stalkers and serial killers have access to the type of technology that only a few years ago would have made James Bond pitch a tent. Think you're safe inside your house? Think again. Whether it's from the house across the street, a hidden microphone in your car, or a camera secretly installed in your bathroom, someone could be watching you right now.

CHAPTER 13

RADIATION SPIES— VAN ECK PHREAKING AND HOMEBREW SIGNALS INTERCEPTION

With a handful of cheap electronic components, anyone who's interested can see what's on your computer screen, even if they're nowhere near it.

THREAT LEVEL

WHAT IS IT?

The air around you is thick with electromagnetic radiation. It's totally harmless at the level of concentration you're used to—it takes a lot to beat up your genes enough for cancer or flipper babies to become an issue. But everything electronic you own puts out a signal, and that signal can be intercepted. With the right equipment and know-how, someone could be reading what's on your computer screen right now.

This is called Van Eck phreaking. *Phreaking* is hacker slang for the signals intelligence (SigInt, if you want to sound like you read a lot of Tom Clancy novels) hobby some nerds acquired in the mid-eighties when they realized they could game the newly computerized telecommunications system with a sequence of tones or clicks. It's evolved to refer to any hack that involves the interception or manipulation of a signal. Phone phreaking was used for low-level toll fraud. So far as anyone knows, Van Eck phreaking isn't something done by civilians, except for engineers with something to prove.

To do it, you need to build a device that can intercept and interpret the electromagnetic signal broadcast by a computer monitor. For about $100, you can get a substandard picture and a twenty-to-forty-foot range; short, but enough for someone parked by the curb in front of your house. As you add cost and sophistication, you can increase the fidelity of the image and extend the range up to half a mile. Military-grade Van Eck interceptors can run into the hundreds of thousands of dollars, but you can build a very effective long-range interceptor for a little under $2,000.

HOW DOES IT WORK?

The principle behind Van Eck phreaking is pretty simple. Your computer monitor, as well as your keyboard and mouse, emit a high-frequency radio signal. If you're old enough, you've seen that signal in action. Remember when your mom used to scramble the television by firing up the blender for another round of margaritas? Van Eck radiation in action!

With a portable monitor (to see what there is to see), a variable oscillator and frequency divider (to let you filter and synchronize incoming signals), an antenna (to capture the signals), and the proper cabling, you can intercept the signals output by pretty much any modern electronic device. Wonder what your neighbor is laughing so hard at on the television? Phreak the signal and find out. Curious about why the woman in the cubicle next door needs to hit her keyboard so hard? Your trusty Van Eck interceptor can recreate those violent keystrokes.

Federal Communication Commission standards require modern electronics to include a small amount of shielding, simply to prevent the interference people in their thirties remember from their childhood. What shielding is there, however, is not enough to prevent eavesdropping.

WHO INVENTED IT AND WHY?

No one invented it. The leakage of electromagnetic radiation from electronics is inevitable. That said, Van Eck isn't just a couple of made-up syllables like "Brangelina" or "Steinbrenner."

Wim van Eck is a Dutch engineer and researcher who demonstrated his method for intercepting and reconstituting electromagnetic signals at the 1985 Securicom convention. The demonstration caused a worldwide fascination with the technique and inspired a generation of high-tech paranoia.

Van Eck's technique wasn't a new thing, but he was the first civilian to do it on the cheap.

The government had known since World War II that any electromagnetic signal could be intercepted and decoded. The National Security Agency even created a classified program related to the control and interception of what at the time were called "Compromising Emissions"—which sounds like something government agencies suffer when they begin puberty.

This program, started in the 1960s and called TEMPEST, developed standards for protecting the electronic assets of the United States government from eavesdropping. The NSA also attempted (and one assumes, succeeded) to develop and deploy their own intercept devices. Indeed, in 1984, a Polish spy was arrested in West Germany. Among his papers was a list of locations ideal for engaging in electronic interception of information from government computers. If the Soviets were able to deploy that kind of technology, it's certain that the West had something similar.

The standards established by TEMPEST are probably still followed by the government today—it's tough to say, as most TEMPEST documents remain classified. However, there are a number of TEMPEST measurement standards that were never part of the classified program. This information allows consumer-grade electromagnetic shielding to be made to U.S. government standards.

WHO'S USING IT TO WATCH YOU?

Probably no one

Seriously. It's a complicated and technically intensive way to spy on someone. Also, most of what you do on the computer is pretty mundane, so the chances that someone would want to watch you do it are slim. If you live near MIT or Caltech or somewhere else engineers are encouraged to indulge their worst impulses, someone may be watching you just for the hell of it.

If you're a government agent, it's more likely. Low cost, hard to prevent, and relatively low tech compared to many forms of electronic intelligence gathering, this kind of eavesdropping was made for poor but obnoxious countries. You can bet Iran and North Korea have homegrown geeks scattered all over the world, holed up in hotels near sensitive buildings, tweaking knobs on an oscillator and trying to pull documents from computer screens in the British Parliament or the Pentagon. Of course, we've got our own geeks doing the same thing to them. We're just doing it from space.

If you work in a highly competitive industry or in defense, this kind of eavesdropping is ideal for industrial espionage. Most government buildings are shielded. Large corporations have shielded rooms, too, with computers that are never allowed out and data that cannot be transferred to another machine. But even so, if you're designing the next long-range bomber or guided-missile system or if you work for an oil company trying to discover new sources of crude, someone may be watching your home computer on the off chance that you send an e-mail with just the right information.

WHY IS IT WATCHING YOU?

If someone is spying on your computer screen, there's all sorts of information they could be capturing. They could be recording every single thing you do. Usernames, passwords, bank account numbers, secret questions, private e-mails—all these things are vulnerable.

It's unlikely the government would use this technique to spy on you. For federal spooks and local police, there are easier ways to gain access to your computer, like getting a warrant and just taking your machine.

Van Eck phreaking is too technically sophisticated and time consuming for your typical criminal. Focusing surveillance on a single person on the chance of acquiring valuable financial data is a long game with low rewards. Sophisticated computer crooks are going to rely on malicious software rather than high-tech surveillance so that they can hit multiple targets at once.

If you've got a stalker willing to resort to this, then you're in trouble. This is an individual with above-average intelligence and technical skill. If you're being stalked by someone with the time, know-how, and money to engage in Van Eck surveillance, chances are you're only a few days away from being tied to a bed in a cabin and forced to write a novel.

WHY SHOULD YOU BE WORRIED ABOUT IT?

The amount of information we trust to our computers is incredible. They are the center of our personal and professional lives. We rely on them to manage our finances and interact with our families. To someone with absolute access to your keyboard and monitor, all of that information is free, and much of it is highly valuable.

It requires a moderate amount of technical skill, but it's cheap and there are tutorials and blueprints online for building an interceptor. It's impossible to detect, and unlikely you'll ever be able to fully defend against it. If someone decides to target you, there's very little you can do about it.

WHAT CAN YOU DO ABOUT IT?

Simple scrambling

There are a number of devices on the market that can be used to at least partially shield your computer—EM-scrambling paint, plexiglass screen covers impregnated with a fine copper mesh, etc. None of these solutions can totally protect your computer; some electromagnetic signal will always leak through.

Lock yourself in a cage

For real top-of-the-line protection, you need to get yourself a Faraday cage. This is a box made of conductive material. Properly constructed, it will block enough of your computer's EM output that not even a military-grade Van Eck interceptor will be able to receive a useful signal.

Faraday rooms are standard issue in facilities that work with materials or devices sensitive to static discharge or electromagnetic radiation. If your company has a server room on-site, chances are it's protected from lightning by a Faraday cage. The walls and ceiling are overlapping sheets of aluminum, iron, or copper, with the seams welded and sealed with EM-resistant gaskets. The whole thing is earthed, sending any signal that hits the wall directly into the ground. You can get a Faraday room built for you for the price of a low-end luxury car.

You can also build one yourself. Copper mesh is probably the most effective material for the price—about $8 per square foot. You'll want several layers of mesh, each with a different opening radius to block as many different wavelengths as possible. The good news is that by the time you're done building your Faraday cage, not only will your computer be fully protected, you won't have any money left to steal. It's a win-win!

CHAPTER 14

HIDDEN CAMERAS, SECRET MICROPHONES, AND BLACK BAG TEAMS—THE MEN IN BLACK ARE ON YOUR TRAIL

If you've managed to annoy the right elements in the government or inspire a vendetta conspiracy in enough of your enemies, you should maybe check all of your teddy bears for hidden cameras.

THREAT LEVEL

WHAT IS IT?

Active surveillance is the practice of placing an individual or group under close observation through the use of listening devices, hidden cameras, and human operatives. It is an expensive and complex method of surveillance, and to do it right requires several trained operatives, high-tech equipment, and a lot of time. If you've managed to merit this kind of surveillance, congratulations! You've pissed off some extremely determined and capable people.

Your phone may be tapped, and your house, car, and office will be bugged with listening devices and cameras. Your car will be tagged with a GPS transmitter. Teams of operatives will follow you everywhere you go. They'll point powerful listening devices at your home.

This kind of surveillance is common in movies. Film heroes often spot tails or find bugs with little difficulty. That's because they are well-trained superhumans with uncanny powers of observation. You are not. In real life, a well-executed tail is extraordinarily difficult to spot, and defeating every form of observation that could be deployed against you requires diligence, time, and skill. You give up valuable intelligence every moment you fail to spot a tail or detect a bug. Your one advantage is that you need neither specialized training nor expensive equipment to beat even a highly trained surveillance team.

It's important to remember that if you've been placed under this kind of surveillance, nothing you do short of faking your death will end the effort. All you can do is remain aware and committed to defeating your observers day after day. Until you address whatever offense you've committed to inspire this kind of effort against you, you better get used to dudes in suits hanging around at the top of your street with parabolic microphones.

HOW DOES IT WORK?

Active surveillance requires a team of at least two people. More likely, you are facing a team of between six and nine. Each member of the surveillance team will have training in breaking and entering, the use of surveillance equipment like hidden cameras and laser microphones, and the techniques of both foot and vehicle tails.

The members of the surveillance team will be of average height and weight, though they may be unusually fit, as they will probably have had some military training. They will dress in clothes appropriate for the situation, avoiding bright colors. They will drive common cars in nondescript hues. If you see them, they will be operating in teams of two or three, but never the same two or three.

This kind of surveillance is set up like an onion, with you at the center. The first layer of the onion is inside your house in the form of remote surveillance devices. The second layer starts on your lawn and extends to the end of the street. In that layer, people crouch in parked vans or behind the dark windows of other buildings, pointing sophisticated and expensive equipment at your windows. The final layer—the one that makes you cry—is the operatives themselves, who will follow you everywhere you go.

The first thing you'll want to worry about is the technology deployed inside your home. Telephone taps have been addressed elsewhere in this book, and are probably not something you need to concern yourself with unless it's a law enforcement agency that's got you under surveillance. What you should be on the lookout for are hidden cameras and microphones.

Cheap (between $100 and $300) and easy to install, hidden cameras or microphones come built into a number of common household objects from smoke alarms to screws. They can be installed in books or stuffed animals or behind mirrors, hidden in a bouquet of flowers or a lamp, plugged into an air freshener, or duct taped to the bottom of a chair or table. Typically, cameras will be motion activated and microphones will be sound activated to avoid wasting battery power. They will be wireless, transmitting any information they capture by radio to a computer in a remote location nearby. If they are installed in an object that plugs into the wall, they will draw their power directly from your home's grid, otherwise they'll be running on batteries that can last weeks on standby.

Your observers may also hide cameras around the exterior of your house, possibly in emergency lights mounted under your neighbor's eaves or drilled into the bottom of a Pepsi can stuck in a hedge. These exterior cameras are intended to catch your comings and goings. Your appearance on an exterior camera will signal the surveillance team to begin a tail.

Just down your street, either in a parked vehicle or another building, members of the surveillance team will be set up with some sophisticated and expensive gear. If you watch football, you're familiar with the parabolic microphone—it's the big, plastic bowl the ESPN interns point at the action on the field. Thanks to the parabolic mike, we get the full football audio experience, complete with grunts, muttering, and the sounds of 600 pounds of flesh colliding at twenty-five miles per hour. Parabolic mikes work on sound the same way radar dishes work on radio—they gather the sound waves in front of them and focus them on a receiver suspended above the center of the dish.

If you're having a meeting with your cohorts, a parabolic mike can pick up the entire conversation without difficulty, but it'll also pick up any ambient noise like music, birds, or a blender. For isolating an individual voice or picking up both ends of a telephone conversation, your enemies will also want a shotgun microphone. With a shotgun mike, an observer can focus on a single sound source a good distance away and capture sound with stunning clarity. Used in conjunction, both kinds of microphones are highly effective intelligence-gathering tools. You can buy a high-end shotgun or parabolic mike for about $400 or you can build your own for about $100. Fortunately, neither microphone works terribly well through barriers, so if you keep your windows closed you're reasonably well protected.

Less conspicuous and with a greater range than either the parabolic or shotgun mike, is the laser microphone. This device fires a laser through your window at some flat surface in your house, reads the vibrations in the surface, and translates those to sound. It can use almost any object in your house as a reflector, including the window through which it is targeted, and can operate at a far greater range than a traditional microphone. If you want a professional-grade one of your very own, expect to spend upwards of $60,000, but you can build one with a shorter range and lower audio fidelity for a couple hundred bucks.

Once you leave your house, the tail begins. Whether you're on foot or in your car, the same basic techniques apply. A three-man team with each individual operating independently will keep you under observation at all times. One man will serve as the "tail," a second as the "eye," and the third as "backup." The roles played by each member of the team will shift constantly without any detectable schedule, making your followers very difficult to spot.

The tail will be the man closest to you, on the same side of the street about a block behind you if you're on foot or one or two cars behind you if you're driving. The eye will be on the other side of the street just behind you on foot or driving next to or just in front of you. The backup will operate parallel to or just behind the tail. As you approach an intersection, the backup man will pass you and turn in the direction opposite the eye. If you continue straight, the backup will become the tail, the tail will become the backup, and the eye will stay in his role. If you turn toward the backup, he will become the tail, the eye will turn and cross the street to become the backup, and the tail will cross the street to become the eye. Turn toward the eye and the backup man becomes the eye, the eye becomes the tail, and the tail becomes the backup. Make sense? Of course not. That's why it's hard to spot. Read this paragraph again and try drawing yourself a picture as you do so. If you do it right, it will look like John Madden went apeshit on the replay with his little light pen, but it may help you visualize.

The tail running scared

If your tail suspects you know you're being followed, they may employ several tactics to throw you off or prevent you from easily losing them. One of the most common is to hire a guy with no training to also follow you. This guy will be obvious and easy to lose. If you think you're being followed by a dude in a Hawaiian shirt, that's the decoy. If you're on foot, the follow team may also have a fourth man in a car in order to maintain the tail should you get in a cab, be picked up by an associate, or get on a bus. Likewise, a car tail may have a fourth man riding as a passenger in one of the cars in order to get out and follow on foot should you leave your vehicle.

The follow team will almost never consist of the same people. A nine-person surveillance team will rotate members of the follow team to ensure that their faces do not become associated in your mind. These people will be smart, capable, and well trained. Good luck getting away from them.

WHO INVENTED IT AND WHY?

No one invented the foot tail or spying. Those are just things people do. Professionals from hunters to spies have always done it in teams. People are nosy for all sorts of reasons, but in the case of a team of highly trained and well-equipped surveillance professionals, the reason is profound and compelling: You have definitely pissed off the absolute worst person you could have pissed off because whomever it is that wants you followed has serious resources.

The microphone was created in 1876 by Emile Berliner. His microphone was intended as a modification to Alexander Graham

Bell's telephone. It was probably first used to spy on people in the 1890s when the government first began tapping people's telephones. Since Berliner's initial invention, countless engineers and inventors have improved on the technology, making it more powerful and compact with every generation.

The motion picture camera was invented more or less at the same time by about thirty different French and English inventors. They all used similar techniques and often even corresponded with each other. Unlike almost every other innovation of the era, the invention of the movie camera seems to have been attended with collaboration and gentlemanly behavior. Probably because Thomas Edison wasn't involved.

As early as the 1940s, Allen Funt was using hidden cameras to punk everyone he could find on national television. At that time, cameras had already been installed in modified fighter planes for the purpose of scouting enemy troop movements, and spies on both sides of the war were busily planting the smallest cameras possible everywhere they could. The modern hidden camera is most commonly known as the nanny cam. Designed primarily to keep a passive eye on the hired help, the nanny cam can easily be adapted to espionage.

The concept of the laser microphone probably originated with the Russian inventor Leon Theremin—famous in the West for the invention of UFO sounds in fifties sci-fi movies. Theremin spent a good portion of his adult life in a Soviet science gulag, inventing all sorts of crazy supertechnology for Stalin, including a technology he called the Buran Bugging System. As early as the mid-forties, Soviet spies were using a laser to spy on the French and American embassies from as far away as 560 yards.

WHO'S USING IT TO WATCH YOU?

The DEA

Federal law enforcement agencies are among the only organizations that can afford to deploy this level of surveillance. The amount of training and the cost of equipment as well as the expense of maintaining a nine-person team over days or weeks of constant surveillance puts an astronomical price tag on these tactics. If the government has placed you under surveillance, they are reasonably sure you are a bad person. You are a gangster or a foreign intelligence agent or a notorious terrorist, and there is probably a kill team on its way to your house right now.

Some truly scary people

If the folks who've placed you under observation are not from the government, then they are not the sort of people you should have messed with. Whatever you did, apologize for it, give back the money, and promise to leave the country. Someone has committed tens of thousands of dollars to watching you. The only kinds of people who do that are supervillains—most normal bad guys would just have you killed. Either you have some kind of extremely valuable information, in which case you should apply to the government for protection, or someone to whom you have access does, in which case you're doomed.

A crazy but highly motivated individual

The flip side of the supervillain coin is the stalker. Stalkers are unable to deploy the full field team, but they may have the wherewithal to bug your house. A dedicated stalker can maintain a decent foot tail and point a shotgun mike at your house. There will be gaps in his information gathering, and once you've discovered and destroyed any bugs he's placed in your home he may not be able to replace them, but he also probably won't care. Stalkers are crazy people with impenetrable motivations and dangerous patterns of behavior. If you've got one, don't bother with the bug hunting and counterespionage—just call the cops.

WHY IS IT WATCHING YOU?

If you are the target of law enforcement, it's because you are not a solo operator. They are looking for information about your criminal contacts, your clients, and your suppliers. Once they have gained enough information to convict you, they will either arrest you or attempt to enlist you as part of their wider surveillance network. You could end up with a microphone taped to your chest and a transmitter digging into the small of your back.

Otherwise, it's because you have something else someone wants. In the case of the rich supervillain, it's probably still information. Perhaps you're the head of a criminal empire and a rival criminal organization has decided to place you under surveillance. If you are a pioneer at the forefront of a high-value industry, this could be corporate espionage. If you're exceedingly wealthy, this may be advance work for a kidnapping or blackmail operation. What do you have that's worth something like $100,000? Whatever it is, that's what your surveillance team is after.

All the lone stalker wants is you. He either wants your unconditional love or to wear your skin and dance around in front of a full-length mirror. Either way, he is gathering intelligence in advance of making a much more aggressive move.

WHY SHOULD YOU BE WORRIED ABOUT IT?

Surveillance of this nature, whether it's the total coverage of the government or the intense yearning of the stalker, is always the precursor to contact or attack. In the case of the government, you will be arrested or pressured to become an informant. In the case of the supervillain, you may be assassinated or kidnapped. In the case of the stalker, you will be thrown into an empty well and threatened with a fire hose unless you put the lotion in the basket.

Unless you are an unusually paranoid or observant person, your watchers are at an advantage. Full-coverage surveillance is hard to spot and takes luck and skill to defeat. You are up against an organization with functionally unlimited resources and a skilled team that outnumbers you nine to one. Be worried because, unless you're aware enough to spot this surveillance, savvy enough to confound it, and lucky enough to end it, the story of your life can only end one way—with you locked in a box and cut off from the world.

WHAT CAN YOU DO ABOUT IT?

Leave the country

Find someplace peaceful and far away and go there. There are some very nice places in the world that do not allow extradition to the United States. Places like Vietnam, Micronesia, and Kuwait. Go relax on a beach, and hope that leaving the country is enough to get whoever it is that's watching you off your back. Whatever it is you have that they want, leave it behind if you can, destroy it if possible, or do your best to travel somewhere you can't be found.

Avoid angering rich criminal masterminds

If you know a guy with Lex Luthor–ish tendencies, don't piss him off. If you're a drug dealer or con man, keep your operation small. If you're pretty, don't be nice to creepy guys. Avoid the notice of the sorts of people who follow folks altogether, and you minimize the risk of finding a snake cam peeking under your bathroom door while you're in the tub.

Drive like a Rhode Islander

Every state likes to brag that they have the worst drivers. It's like a point of perverse pride—especially in the Northeast—to claim that drivers in certain cities or counties are just the most inconsiderate, insane vehicular-homicidal maniacs in the world. The truth is, people in most states are pretty okay drivers. The one exception is Rhode Island.

Rhode Island has one speed limit—ramming speed. Stop lights are considered optional, and stop signs are better if ignored completely. Turn signals are considered a sign of weakness. State law allows a bag limit of three elderly pedestrians and one cyclist per season. Bus drivers and cabbies get most of their leisure reading done at work. The state flag actually shows a person texting while driving, and the state bird is a middle finger extended from a driver's side window. No one in Rhode Island is ever followed, because following a crazy person is nigh impossible.

If you want to spot a car tail, pretend you're in Rhode Island.

- Speed through yellow lights (or, better yet, stop on yellow and floor it the moment it turns red).
- If you must signal, signal the direction opposite your intended turn.
- Turn late, drive the wrong way down one-way streets, pull into underground parking lots, and just drive around for a while.
- Double-park, get out of your car, and walk around the block.
- Behave like a completely insane asshole.

Anyone who goes out of his way to mimic you is your tail.

Once you've spotted your tail, memorize the car, the license plate number, and, if possible, the face of the driver. A license plate number and Google can be a powerful weapon in your arsenal, but nothing beats knowing the face of one of the members of your surveillance team. Since you're driving like a jerk anyway, take a picture of the guys following you—nothing makes a spy angrier than having his picture taken.

Once you've spotted your tail, the red-light trick, the one-way street trick, and parking garages with multiple exits can be powerful tools for losing them. Be ready for your drive to take a lot longer than you planned, however. Spotting and losing a tail takes time and patience.

A lot of these tactics can help you spot and lose a foot tail as well. Watch the opposite side of the street in the reflection of shop windows. Take unpredictable, circuitous routes, keeping a close eye on the faces of pedestrians around you. Ignore the obvious decoys—making an effort to lose those guys will alert your tail that you know you're being followed. Sudden U-turns and unscheduled stops in local businesses can be helpful. Duck into places like biker bars and goth clubs, where your tail will stand out. Buy a ticket to a movie and leave the theater immediately through an emergency exit. Make a habit of remembering every face you see—the ones you see over and over again are possible tails.

Move to a cul-de-sac

Surveillance teams hate cul-de-sacs. Tail cars and other unfamiliar vehicles are easy to spot, the neighbors all know each other, and unknown pedestrians never just wander down them. If there's an empty house on your cul-de-sac and nine dudes all move into it together, that's your surveillance team.

Buy a bug detector

For about $200, you can buy a gadget for finding spy equipment. Bug detectors are basically radio frequency scanners. As you sweep the antenna around the room, they hunt for the transmissions being broadcast by any cameras or microphones hidden in the room. Remember that cameras are often motion activated and microphones are typically sound activated; turn on your stereo and the lights before doing your sweep.

Once detected, you will still need to find the bug. Look for objects with line of sight to a large area of the room—these may have cameras installed in them. If there's a phone in the room, check it for microphones first, and then sweep outwards. A mirror designed to hide a camera will appear partially transparent under close inspection with a flashlight.

Once you've found the bug, you have a few options. You can destroy it, which will be satisfying but will also alert the surveillance team that you're aware of them. Far more fun is turning it against your observers, either by feeding false information to them or by giving them more than they bargained for. Make them watch you dance naked.

If you think you know what the surveillance team is after, this may be an opportunity to do away with them. Use their surveillance devices to feed them a plausible but false version of the information they seek; it may be enough to get them off your back. This tactic takes some planning and a good deal of time, but if you can casually provide them with all they think they need, they may back off.

Make some noise

Exterior microphones, especially parabolic and laser mikes, can be defeated by ambient noise. For the parabolic mike, all you really need to do is crank some music, turn on a blender, or hire a guy with a keytar to jam as you speak. Laser mikes are a little better at resolving the human voice from background noise. To be absolutely certain, you'll want to buy some custom-made laser-mike jammers for about $100 (per window). These little machines stick to your windows and put out white noise in the same frequency as the human voice, making it impossible for a laser mike to isolate your voice from the background. Alternatively, you can attach other noisemakers to your windows—things like sonic toothbrushes, small fans, or, if you're feeling saucy, vibrators work great. These common household objects may not work as well as a purpose-built jammer, but they will save you some money.

Shotgun mikes are a little harder to jam. They can target individual sources of sound from hundreds of feet away, so ambient noise is useless. A wall, however, is a pretty efficient means of blocking their audio pickup. If you're going to have a sensitive conversation, do it in an interior room, away from windows, and almost any form of remote audio pickup will be useless.

Hire your own team

If you've got the money, this is a great solution. Your own team of trained surveillance professionals will sweep your house for bugs, scout the surrounding location for observers, and run interference against any possible tail when you decide to go out. These guys come with all the tech you need to defeat various types of listening devices or hidden cameras, and they will have the same level of training as their opponents.

The risk here is that the person employing the team watching you will have hired or co-opted other organizations as well. Vet each member of your team carefully; infiltration is always a danger. Just because you're paying these guys doesn't mean you can trust them.

Avoid patterns

Established patterns are the surveillance professional's best friend. Most people do more or less the same thing every day. They get up, eat the same breakfast, get in the same car, and drive the same route to work. These patterns are the comforting trappings of daily life without which most of us would quickly cease functioning. But they also make it easy for anyone—even an amateur—to keep us under observation.

If you're worried about watchers, don't establish predictable patterns. Rent cars instead of owning. Avoid becoming a regular visitor to a single place. If you have to go to the same place every day, like work, take a different route every time you go. Randomly mix up modes of transportation—bike, bus, drive, or walk. Make life hard on your observers by never doing the same thing twice. The trick here is to make life as stressful for a surveillance team as possible. The more you make them work, the more exhausted they get, and the more mistakes they are likely to make.

SECURITY CAMERAS— EYES, EYES EVERYWHERE

They're everywhere. They perch on top of traffic lights, hang in the corners of restaurants and offices, lurk behind the mirrors of dressing rooms, and sleep comfortably in the pockets of almost every person in the country. Cameras never blink, never get tired, and never stop watching you.

THREAT LEVEL

WHAT IS IT?

Closed-circuit television cameras are the type of surveillance with which most of us are most familiar—and most comfortable. We've lived most of our lives under the eyes of cameras hidden behind little black domes in ceilings or bolted in clusters to the corners of buildings. The presence of CCTV cameras has become so ubiquitous as to be comforting—a darkened parking lot is filled with menace until we notice the security cameras keeping watch over us. The surveillance of public space is an accepted and even welcomed thing.

In recent years, however, cameras have multiplied to occupy niches in almost every part of our lives. They've been mounted behind the mirrors in dressing rooms and in the corners of public bathrooms. They hang from the ceilings of our places of work. They're mounted in the dashboards of police cruisers and atop our computer screens. Everyone around you is carrying one, and many of them live with their fingers on the record button, just in case something interesting happens.

The increasing omnipresence of cameras is not an illusion. More than 4 million security cameras are currently in operation in the United Kingdom. In the United States, the number is probably even higher. From the moment you leave the house in the morning to the moment you lock the door behind you in the evening, there will be very few gaps in the video record of your day. If you are in a car accident or a fight, attention becomes even more intense as dozens of bystanders pull out their cell phones to take video.

There was a time when all of these cameras existed just to protect us or guard the sanctity of our high-value property. Now, they exist mostly to guard the petty property of department stores from minor theft, to catch us speeding, or to record us at our worst. Sometime in the recent past, cameras graduated from saving us from the worst elements of society to attempting to catch us behaving poorly or foolishly. Most of the cameras around us are not operated in the hope of stopping a kidnapper; they're there in the hope of scoring a YouTube hit by recording you getting hit in the crotch with a cricket bat.

For the most part, privacy concerns about the increasing prevalence of security cameras and the knee-jerk tendency of the citizenry to videotape everything have been ignored. In the UK, CCTV cameras are supposed to be registered and regulated by a public authority, but compliance with that law is spotty. In the United States, it's considered good form to tell people when they might be videotaped changing their clothes, and surveillance systems in dressing rooms aren't supposed to be able to record anything, but there's no verification requirement. Some police organizations have tried to make it illegal to videotape police in the course of their work, but those efforts have largely failed. The general rule that seems to be taking shape over the last decade is that anything you do outside your house is fair game—if you're willing to do it in front of your neighbors, you should be prepared to do it in front of the entire Internet.

HOW DOES IT WORK?

The term *closed-circuit television* refers to any television or video camera that delivers the content it records to a single, specific location or group of locations (a hard drive or bank of video screens). Theoretically, a CCTV system is a closed system, impossible to access from the outside (though that is less true than it once was). Hard drives or other memory devices can be internal to the camera, and can record days or weeks of footage.

These days, CCTV cameras often use known network protocols to transmit information to their storage or display media. That's a fancy way of saying that the video feed from many cameras travels—unsecured and unencrypted—over the Internet to wherever it will be reviewed. Some cameras openly display their video feed online, either by design or by accident. Others can be hacked fairly easily.

Most of the other cameras we find ourselves commonly surrounded by operate on a similar principle. Cell phone and digital cameras record still photos or video directly to an internal memory device. Most cell phones and some digital cameras are capable of then transmitting that content to other devices or a website. Similarly, webcams record video and deliver the content to a computer hard drive or website or simply provide a live feed to the operator. Don't be fooled into believing that just because a webcam is attached to your computer you're the only operator.

For the most part, footage from a given camera is owned by the owner of the camera. If you are recorded in a public place or on the property of another person, the video record of your passing belongs to them. Your entry into a public space or a private space owned by another person constitutes permission. Privately, they are free to do whatever they want with whatever images of you they capture.

However, if they decide to begin posting things on the Internet, the law becomes more vague. Unless you're doing something newsworthy—as vague and meaningless a word as there ever could be—you pretty much own the rights to your likeness. If you've been filmed without your permission and the owner of the film is realizing a profit, you have the right to demand a part of that profit or the removal of the video from wherever it's being shown. If the video is painfully embarrassing and recorded somewhere you should have had the reasonable expectation of privacy (your high school AV room, for instance, or a friend's bathroom), you'd be within your rights to demand compensation or the removal of the video or both.

WHO INVENTED IT AND WHY?

CCTV was invented in 1942 by a German engineer named Walter Bruch. He designed and invented the system for the Nazis after they realized that making dudes stand directly under their V-2 rockets to watch them take off was an impractical way of reviewing performance. Remote television cameras offered an elegant alternative. Using information from the video feed, Germany was able to refine the performance of their rockets well enough to send them zipping happily all over Europe for three years.

CCTV systems were deployed for security purposes in U.S. government installations in the 1950s, but the first public deployment wasn't until the late sixties, when Olean (the fat-free city!), New York, installed them along their main street in an attempt to fight crime. Around the same time, banks and shops began wondering what life would be like if there was some kind of technology that allowed them to surreptitiously photograph the people who robbed them. By the early seventies, CCTV was everywhere.

The first camera phones hit the market in the late-nineties. Over the intervening decade or so, digital camera technology has gotten smaller, faster, and sharper, until today, when high-definition video can make its way instantly from your fist to Facebook.

Your webcam works more or less exactly like your phone camera. The destination of the video feed from the camera is dependent on the software running the camera. If you're using an IP telephony program like Skype, the feed is delivered to another person's computer, where it could be recorded fairly easily (the legality of such a recording being dependent on the locations of both interlocutors). Your webcam can also be set to deliver a continuous feed to a website or simply record everything it sees to your hard drive. Depending on your computer's setup, your camera could also be activated remotely from another machine, either through malicious software or a totally benign network connection.

WHO'S USING IT TO WATCH YOU?

Everyone in the world

You are never outside the range of someone's camera. We've grown so used to being under observation that sharing our appearance, location, and status has become second nature. Many cameras these days even include features that make it easier to take a picture of yourself as well as date stamping and geolocation features. No longer do you have to wait for other people to record you being an idiot—beat them all to the punch and post your own concussion to YouTube.

Security guards scrutinize your every move. Cops review your license plate for outstanding warrants. Your behavior is observed by your boss. Complete strangers watch and wait for you to do something worth recording. Video surveillance is everywhere, and it is being monitored by everyone.

WHY IS IT WATCHING YOU?

Back in the day, CCTV surveillance came in two flavors. There was the kind that kept you safe—it watched you in parking garages, banks, and empty streets. The hope of those cameras was that their presence would frighten away criminals. The promise was that, even if the criminals still came, they would be seen and caught. Then there was the other kind, which watched the perimeters of places where barbed wire and dogs weren't enough. Antsy soldiers and armed guards watched the feeds from these cameras waiting for someone who needed shooting to wander into their field of vision.

Those two types of camera still exist, but far more prevalent in the realm of security cameras these days is the one that is watching you for any sign of mischief. These are the video camera equivalent of the horrible old lady in your neighborhood who used to scream at you from her porch. She was never sure what you were up to, but she was certain it was naughty, whatever it was. The assumption behind the installation of most security cameras nowadays is that everyone is out to rip someone off; that, by and large, society is just a collection of savage beasts held barely in check by the threat of punishment.

Without constant video surveillance, civilization would collapse in an orgy of pilfered candy bars and stolen underwear.

And then, of course, there's the profit motive. Private citizens record everything because they believe they have something to gain. Catch something funny enough on your phone, and you just might end up with a bit part in the next Zach Galifianakis movie. Post the right kind of hilarity on Funnyordie and you stand to make thousands. At the very least, people might bookmark your YouTube channel. Internet fame isn't much, but it's enough that most people witnessing a car accident will think to videotape first and help second.

WHY SHOULD YOU BE WORRIED ABOUT IT?

In September of 2010, two students at Rutgers University—Molly Wei and Dharun Ravi—used a webcam to surreptitiously stream a video of Ravi's roommate Tyler Clementi hooking up with another man. Ravi invited his followers on Twitter to join him in watching his roommate be gay—which, when you think about it, is a pretty gay way to make fun of someone for being gay.

This invasion of privacy almost certainly contributed to Celementi's decision, a few days later, to jump to his death from the George Washington Bridge.

What Ravi and Wei did was illegal—they could each face as much as ten years in prison—but it was not uncommon or difficult. Most of the camera lenses around you lie dormant, waiting for the chance to catch you doing something strange or humiliating. In most cases, those incidents will not occur in a private bedroom, but in the public sphere, where the law is much more loose about what can and cannot be recorded and distributed on the Internet.

Ravi and Wei were only caught because they offered to share the video feed of Clementi's hookup. Had they simply recorded the video for their own use, it would still have been illegal, but they never would have been caught. Anyone with access to your computer could do the same. Video captured in this manner could easily be distributed anonymously at a later date or used privately as blackmail material.

Of course, the quiet brutality of this act is only the symptom of a deeper issue. As video surveillance has become more and more prevalent, we have become more comfortable with it. The expectation of privacy has decreased. We are annoyed, but not shocked, that we might be caught partially naked on camera while we try on pants at the department store. We experience a mild sense of injustice by video surveillance at our place of work when our parents would have been sickened.

The private realms into which video surveillance is expanding represent a loss of our right to privacy. Our movements around the city or the nation can now be tracked from camera to camera. Facial recognition technology makes it easier than ever before for the police or a corporation to know, step by step, the routes we take from place to place. The more time we spend on camera, the less time we spend as free individuals.

WHAT CAN YOU DO ABOUT IT?

Ask nicely

If you see someone about to begin videotaping you, ask them nicely to stop. Depending on where you are, your refusal of permission may be enough to compel someone to quit sticking a camera in your face. If they refuse, you may be able to prosecute. Also, you know, some people still respond properly to civility.

Stay home

There's not much you can do about the cameras posted at every intersection in some cities, in the bank, the 7-11, or the mall. The best you can hope to do is stay out of their field of vision. The easiest way to do that is to simply stay home. If you don't go outside, they can't catch you on tape.

Of course, that's not really practical for most people. So you can also choose to be a little crazy. Get yourself a pad, pencil, and detailed map of your hometown. Keep notes on the locations of cameras and their fields of vision. You can minimize your exposure by planning your routes around those cameras. It's not a simple task, but it can be done.

The same tactic can be used for businesses you frequent. Track the placement and sight lines of all the cameras you can see. There will often be blind spots in CCTV set-ups. Stick to those blind spots as much as possible. You'll look like a maniac shuffling around the edges of rooms, but at least you'll stay reasonably anonymous.

Move to Africa

A functioning, omnipresent network of CCTV cameras requires reliable, uninterrupted power. The third world is famous for, among other things, unreliable power grids. The only places in most of Africa that have CCTV cameras are installations with independent power supplies. Not only that, but cell phone penetration in Africa is only about 21 percent, and many of those are prepaid phones without cameras. Also, in most of the third world, people in general don't go around randomly videotaping each other anyway, because it's a really excellent way to get shot.

CHAPTER 16

419S, PHISHERMEN, AND HACKERS— WHO'S PWNING YOU RIGHT NOW

Organized crime on the Internet has made a very good living for itself by ripping off the unwary. Traditional con games have made the leap into the computer age, turning what used to be the art of the con into an assembly-line process. On any given day, someone, somewhere, is trying to rip you off, and it all starts with a simple e-mail.

THREAT LEVEL

WHAT IS IT?

The Internet is like a bad neighborhood in a big city. Sure, that's where all the good clubs are, the porn is cheap, and you can get something to eat late at night. But that's also where all the muggers, drug dealers, and con men hang out.

The ultimate aim of most online assaults is the acquisition of cash, but these are not simple robberies; they are complex scams perpetrated by large, organized groups, designed to inflict the maximum amount of chaos and ruin on their victims. Should you be unfortunate enough to fall victim to one of the many forms of online fraud, you stand to lose everything—your money, your home, even your identity. Your computer could be co-opted without your knowledge into an ersatz network of automated cyberwar soldiers. They target not just individuals, but entire corporations and even countries.

If movies are to be believed, your average hacker is a single, socially retarded genius working from his parents' basement, amusing himself by inflicting his worst impulses on an unsuspecting public. He is able to type with such uncanny speed that the networks of entire governments give way beneath his mighty skills. In this, as in so many other things, movies lie.

Identity theft, fraud, and malicious hacks are big businesses, worth billions of dollars a year. The organizations that perpetrate these crimes are Russian mob fronts, Nigerian narcoterrorist gangs, and rogue elements of the Chinese government. These are serious, world-class villains, the kinds of guys who ride around in convoys of armored Mercedes SUVs guarded by burly ex-Spetsnaz beefcakes armed with MP5 submachineguns. They kidnap tourists, kill politicians, sponsor terrorism, run human trafficking rings, and operate child porn networks. Online fraud and identity theft are not the only businesses in which they involve themselves, but these are the ones that grease the financial wheels and keep the rest of the operation running.

The e-mails that initiate most online scams originate from cubicle farms not unlike the one in which you probably work. The management structure is similar to your company, with code monkeys and administrative grunts doing most of the initial work—tracking potential victims, harvesting e-mail addresses, and composing and sending the original e-mail. The only difference is that you have a 401(k) and health care, while the retirement plan from a Nigerian 419 scam organization is more likely a bullet to the brain.

Make no mistake. The people out there trying to rip you off are experienced, intelligent, and either desperate or highly motivated. They will attack you from multiple angles and will keep trying until they get you. If they can't take your identity, they'll take your money, and if they can't get to that they'll go after your computer and link it to their network of spam-distributing robot slaves. Your only defense is knowledge and a healthy bit of paranoia.

HOW DOES IT WORK?

By far the simplest and most common scam is known as phishing. In a phishing scam, the victim receives what appears to be a legitimate e-mail from a trusted financial institution or social networking site requesting a verification of account numbers, user names, passwords, or other sensitive information. Often, the e-mail will include a link to what appears to be the actual website of the organization.

Once you enter whatever information is requested into this fake website, the scammer will quickly hijack your account, stripping it of everything valuable—credit card numbers, bank account information, social security number, and cash. Anything of immediate value, like credit cards and bank accounts, goes into the pocket of the scammer. Identity information enters a vast black market trolled by terrorists, drug smugglers, and spies.

More sophisticated phishers have done their homework, using relatively simple software to deduce which banks and credit cards you actually use. A few years ago, it was all spam, using the letterhead of a popular bank or other service in the hope that some proportion of potential targets would actually be clients. Now, phishing e-mails are targeted; you can count on a clever con man to already know where you bank before he contacts you.

Phishing is a short game with a huge earning potential, but it's also fairly easy to spot. Your bank won't send you an e-mail with a bunch of misspellings in it, and even if they did, they would never ask you for this kind of information. Your bank already knows your name and account number because they're your bank. Many victims notice fairly quickly that fraudulent charges are being made against their credit cards or unauthorized withdrawals are being made from their bank account. If you're fast, you can often stop the theft before significant damage is done.

The longer game, with even greater potential earnings, is the one in which the victim is convinced to eagerly hand over his money. Most commonly known as a Nigerian 419 scam (for the part of the Nigerian criminal code that supposedly governs such fraud), this is a variation on older traditional con games.

It begins with an e-mail—usually from someone claiming to be a relative or agent of a deposed African prince, discredited politician, or down-on-his-luck oil baron. The e-mail will weave a tale of the unjust imprisonment of a beloved ruler, and obscene wealth secured just out of reach of the relative or agent—wealth he is willing to share with the person kind enough to offer assistance. For a small initial investment of only a few thousand dollars, the victim is assured to receive tens of millions of dollars in return.

The initial e-mail is like those big yellow envelopes the Publisher's Clearinghouse used to send out promising millions of dollars in cash and prizes. It draws you in with a promise of millions, and secures your trust with the smiling face of Ed McMahon. If you're foolish enough to reply to one of these e-mails, you can look forward to a long, complicated e-mail relationship in which the con man will appeal to every emotion you have. He will make you feel guilt for prolonging the captivity of the poor African prince; impatience for the vast wealth you're about to receive; and affection for your new Nigerian friend.

Inevitably, once you have wired him the first few thousand dollars, complications will arise, requiring more funding. A skilled and aggressive scammer can keep you going until you're cleaned out. They will encourage you to tap your relatives and friends for funds.

Sometimes, when your financial resources are completely drained, he will encourage you to come visit him to meet and receive the thanks of the happily freed sovereign. Upon your arrival, you may be kidnapped and held for ransom or simply murdered.

Phishing and 419 scamming are arts that require time, skill, and a ruthless sensibility. They are vastly profitable, but not necessarily for everyone. Some business models resort to a more brute-force style. If the 419 scam is the Internet equivalent of being gently swindled at a Monaco casino, malicious software is like being mugged by the Internet.

Malicious software comes in numerous forms, and can be deployed in a number of ways. Viruses are self-replicating programs primarily designed to inflict maximum chaos and damage on the largest number of computers as quickly as possible. Worms replicate and move from machine to machine, but rarely do direct damage to individual machines or networks; instead, they deliver a payload to a target computer, usually something designed to allow a remote operator permanent access to the machine.

Viruses can wreak untold damage, but the typical loss is only information. They can cost corporations and governments millions in labor, data recovery, and equipment replacement, but they rarely have the far-reaching consequences of the far more insidious worm.

Viruses and worms are typically deployed through malicious e-mails, links on websites, or simply as apps that run as soon as an infected website is accessed. They can also be loaded as Trojan programs into files downloaded from peer-to-peer networks or other legitimate-seeming pieces of software. Worms can enslave your computer, forcing it to work as part of a remotely operated malicious network known as a botnet.

Without your knowledge, your computer could be engaging in the distribution of spam, the serving of illegal or pirated software, or a concentrated attack on a corporate or government network. It could also be remembering your passwords, account names and numbers, and e-mail addresses. It is almost certainly copying and distributing itself to your friends and coworkers. Even as it subverts your machine to do the bidding of its evil masters, it is quietly delivering your identity into their hands.

WHO INVENTED IT AND WHY?

The modern con game began with a Spanish prisoner. As far back as the 1870s, American businessmen began receiving letters from Cuba, Spain, and South America claiming to be from European military officers or aristocrats wrongly imprisoned in Spain. These men claimed to have heard of the American man from a mutual acquaintance, who will also have recommended an agent to mediate the transaction between the "prisoner" and the mark.

The prisoner has, sadly, a beautiful young daughter—his heir and only offspring—as well as a large sum of money that is inaccessible to the daughter, the agent, and the prisoner. The prisoner's only wish is that some honest man will undertake to retrieve the money and bring the daughter and her fortune to the United States. In exchange, the man performing this service will receive one-third of the fortune and management of the rest in the name of the beautiful, young, and now rich, daughter (who, it is implied, will soon require a husband). The prisoner beseeches the victim to contact the agent, who will only need a small sum of money in order to claim the fortune and secure passage for it and the daughter to the United States.

So successful has this con been that it has been run with little variation for more than a century. E-mail has just made it easier. Every other scam on the Internet has its roots, more or less, in the tradition of the Spanish Prisoner and other less well-known cons.

Phishing, like any good con, relies on the essentially trusting nature of most people. Its roots lie in the earliest days of the Internet as we now know it, when America Online was still a thing that people used instead of just a footnote in the Wikipedia entry for "Good Ideas Poorly Executed." Originally, phishing took the form of an instant message sent over the AOL network that appeared to be from an official source. Passwords or payment details would be requested, and the result was usually a hacked account or some minor credit card fraud. Inside the relatively closed architecture of AOL, phishing on the scale it is practiced now wasn't really possible. It wasn't until the populace at large began to migrate online that phishing really took off.

The concept of computer viruses and other self-replicating software was originated by the mathematician John von Neumann. Von Neumann will be familiar to science fiction nerds as the guy who first realized the human race would eventually be wiped out by self-replicating killer robots. He theorized that any sufficiently automated system could easily make a copy of itself in much the same way an organic virus does.

The first true computer virus appeared in 1971 on the military network known as ARPANET. Creeper, written by researcher Bob Thomas, was created only as an experiment, and was destroyed as quickly as it was built. ARPANET, along with its vulnerable architecture, would eventually become the Internet we all know and love.

The original infection vector for malicious software was by floppy disk. Which means, you know, you were kind of a software whore if you got a virus back in those days. You shouldn't be inserting other people's floppies into your drive slot unless you have protection. It wasn't until the World Wide Web exploded that malware became big business. With the increase in connection speeds and web traffic and e-mail, the distribution and management of illicit software became simple.

WHO'S USING IT TO WATCH YOU?

The Russian Business Network

The Russian Business Network is a large, illegal corporation run by a bunch of anonymous psychopaths. It is probably based in St. Petersburg, Russia, but likely has affiliates around the world. They engage in everything from child pornography to running one of the largest and most dangerous botnets on the planet. They deal in new identities for terrorists, and rent out their services to other organizations that need to orchestrate cyberwar-style attacks. The RBN is also notorious for having no sense of humor whatsoever. They are serious assholes with millions of dollars at their command, software that not even the FBI can kill, and a global reach. They are organized, wealthy, intelligent, and totally ruthless.

Nigerian narcoterrorists

These dudes are slightly less terrifying than the Russian Business Network, but only because their reach isn't as long, and they're honestly just not as bright. They do, however, occasionally murder people. The identity of a recently dead person is an ideal cover for running drugs or operating an international credit card scam. If they can lure a mark in a 419 scam into their clutches, they will hold him for ransom until the money is exhausted, and then they will kill him and profit from his identity.

Enemy nations

Large, powerful botnets will be a critical weapon in the next war fought between nation states. Without question, the United States, Russia, China, various European countries, and probably North Korea and others have extremely powerful worms ready to go. There's little evidence of it, but it's entirely plausible that these worms have already been deployed and quietly infect millions of computers, only to be activated the moment a war is declared. These are the nukes of the Internet age; on a moment's notice, thousands or millions of computers could suddenly be tasked with crippling or destroying the information infrastructure of another nation.

This has already happened. The 2010 attack on Google and dozens of other companies in China was almost certainly military, judging from its sophistication. The governments of Estonia and Georgia were brought nearly to their knees by botnet attacks that may have originated at least partially with the Russian military. South Korea may have been attacked by a North Korean botnet in 2009. Your computer may already be a part of a botnet operated by the U.S. government and tasked with taking down the network of the next country to announce it has a lot of oil.

WHY IS IT WATCHING YOU?

In the case of a scam or malware operation run by a criminal organization, you are being watched in the hope that you can be ripped off. Regardless of their sophistication, the people who run these operations are little more than thugs. They care about nothing other than their next dollar, and they will do anything they can to squeeze it out of you.

Governments aren't trying to steal your identity or financial information, they just want to draft your computer in the next big war. Planning for big wars is one of those things governments do, even when the likelihood of there ever being one is slim to none. This is not to say that military malware couldn't be repurposed to spy on you, just that it's probably not doing so at the moment.

WHY SHOULD YOU BE WORRIED ABOUT IT?

The most common and serious danger presented by any of these threats is identity theft. Identity theft often goes unnoticed until serious damage is done, and the consequences can be dire and difficult to untangle. It's tough to even know when or how your identity was compromised. It can cost you thousands of dollars, destroy your credit rating, and if it goes unnoticed long enough, end in serious legal trouble for you and your family.

In some cases, if an identity is going to be used to cover a criminal or terrorist action, it is helpful for the original owner of an identity to disappear or die suddenly. This does not happen often, but it is not unheard of, and the organizations that stand to gain the most from trade in reliable fake identities would certainly not hesitate to kill someone if it meant making a little extra cash.

The worms that infect your computer, capture information, and enslave it to a botnet can corrupt files and even disable or destroy hardware. They are insidious, difficult to detect, and often impossible to destroy. Military-grade software is fantastically complex and obscenely powerful, and no consumer-grade antivirus software has a hope against it. Even the stuff fielded by the Russian mafia is pretty top of the line—Internet security companies are in an ongoing war against large online criminal organizations. Many of them even regularly fend off active assaults on their own networks.

The criminals that prey on those wandering the wild Internet are determined, intelligent, well funded, well equipped, and vicious. They exist in fluid, anonymous organizations that can disappear in an instant, reinvent themselves, and be back online within hours.

WHAT CAN YOU DO ABOUT IT?

Don't be an idiot

Most Internet cons rely on the naiveté of the mark. Treat the Internet as you would any reasonably questionable neighborhood. Do not trust strangers. If a deal seems too good to be true, it certainly is. If you doubt the legitimacy of an e-mail from a bank or other organization, try calling the organization or e-mailing them directly to ask about it.

If the guy writing you the letter was really a bank official or a Nigerian king (or even the friend of a Nigerian king), he would know how to spell words in English. You know where African kings go to college? The United States. They don't misspell things, especially when they write e-mails offering millions of dollars to people. They take that shit seriously. If a letter is in broken English, it's a scam.

Never pay for anything that is advertised as "free." Never give a bank account or routing number to an individual or an obscure foreign organization. Never hand out your name, your social security number, or your address to a stranger. Don't go to Nigeria to meet a prince.

When you get a phishing or 419 e-mail, report it to the FBI or Secret Service. Both organizations run task forces and share information on combating the groups that run these scams. The more information they have, the more effective their efforts will be.

If you do get conned, don't be too proud to go to the authorities. As soon as you realize you've been had, report what has happened to the FBI or the Secret Service. If you kept a record of your correspondence with the scammer, send it all to the authorities. They may not be able to recover everything you lost, but they will be able to help you avoid further loss and give you advice on how to protect your identity.

Use a reputable virus-scanning software

And when I say reputable, I mean one recommended by a friend, with a name you recognize. The Russians may not have much of a sense of humor, but their sense of irony is extremely well developed. One of their favorite ways to distribute malware is through fake virus-detection software. If you don't have any friends, go to the computer store closest to your house and ask the first person you see without a Russian accent what antivirus program he recommends.

CONCLUSION

Unless you've been living in a cave for the last twenty years, it's too late for you to do anything about the erosion of your privacy. Too much money and power has been put into spying on everyone all the time for you to be able to totally remove yourself from the spotlight. Too many cool toys and hot deals have been offered in exchange for little pieces of your private life. Criminals have learned too many lessons and gotten way too smart.

No one out there is interested in protecting you. If a corporation offers to hide you from its competitors, it's only to sell you to its friends. If the government promises to keep you safe, it's only so you can be pumped full of LSD and locked in a pitch-black room. When a stranger offers to shake your hand, it's only to steal your rings. The only person actually interested in making sure you're safe and happy is you.

Time and technology are on the side of the spies. For every new bit of convenience, for every point of contact between you and the outside world, you sacrifice one more tiny sliver of your privacy. As long as there is money to be made off of you, you will remain a target. You will be pressured from every angle to volunteer, to share, to sacrifice, or to sign up.

Ultimately, you decide how much of yourself gets shared with the world. You need not cut yourself off from the modern age in order to live safely and privately, protected both from the corporations that want to exploit you and the criminals that hope to victimize you. You need only put some small measure of thought into who—and what—has access to your life. Consume, communicate, and connect with care, rather than blindly hurling yourself out into the world.

The next time you are asked to give up some piece of personal information, ask yourself this question: Who stands to profit? Who benefits from your sacrifice? Is it you? Or is it a stranger with one hand extended in friendship and the other reaching for your wallet?

INDEX

DAILY BENDER

Want Some More?

Hit up our humor blog, The Daily Bender, to get your fill of all things funny—be it subversive, odd, offbeat, or just plain mean. The Bender editors are there to get you through the day and on your way to happy hour. Whether we're linking to the latest video that made us laugh or calling out (or bullshit on) whatever's happening, we've got what you need for a good laugh.

If you like our book, you'll love our blog. (And if you hated it, "man up" and tell us why.) Visit The Daily Bender for a shot of humor that'll serve you until the bartender can.

Sign up for our newsletter at

www.adamsmedia.com/blog/humor

and download our Top Ten Maxims No Man Should Live Without.